1981

W9-CMI-036

Descartes /

3 0301 00056585 9

DESCARTES

JONATHAN RÉE

DESCARTES

LIBRARY
College of St. Francis
JOLIET, ILL.

PICA PRESS
NEW YORK

Published in the United States of America in 1975
by Pica Press
Distributed by Universe Books
381 Park Avenue South, New York, N.Y. 10016

Copyright © Jonathan Rée, 1974

*All rights reserved. No part of this publication
may be reproduced, stored in a retrieval system, or
transmitted, in any form or by any means, electronic,
mechanical, photocopying, recording, or otherwise,
without the prior permission of the publishers.*

Library of Congress Catalog Card Number: 74-27243

ISBN 0-87663-717-9

Printed in the United States of America

194.1
R32 2

Acknowledgements

Ross Carlisle, Barbara Coysh
Asta Fink, Hans Fink, Harry Frankfurt
Benjamin Gibbs, Anthony Kenny
Judy Mabro, Gwynneth Matthews, John Mepham
Ursula Owen, Mark Platts
Bob Sutcliffe, Janet Vaux
John Wolfers

94902

Analytical Contents

7

Analytical Contents

He thought that in the case of human beings this gland contained something non-physical – the soul. (The 'homunculus' concept of the soul.)

In his early writings, Descartes claimed that the soul perceives and acts only on certain states of the brain, which he called 'ideas'.

In the works of some later philosophers this concept of ideas developed into the empiricist theory of mind (or ideas).

This theory could not serve the purposes for which Descartes designed the concept of ideas.

6 DOUBT AND THE SOUL

Descartes's philosophy changed considerably in about 1630.

Descartes's late philosophy is based on the method of doubt, a technique for identifying the essences of things.

The method of doubt corresponds to analysis.

Descartes tried to identify the essence of the soul, beginning with the *cogito*, which shows that it is senseless to doubt that one is thinking.

The concept of mind differs from that of the soul in that it is closely associated with that of thought.

Descartes argued (a) that one can doubt the existence of everything except one's mind without doubting the existence of one's soul and (b) that it followed that the mind is identical with the soul (the idealist definition of the soul).

7 DESCARTES'S LATE CONCEPT OF IDEAS

The Platonistic dualism of sensory and intellectual knowledge was almost universally subscribed to up to Descartes's time.

Descartes relied on it in some early writings.

But in his late writings he rejected it.

This led to two enormous advances in the theory of knowledge: (a) Descartes came to treat ideas as mental rather than physical, and this enabled him to disentangle the notion of ideas from the empiricist theory.

(b) Descartes generalized the notion of ideas, and this enabled him to use it in explaining both intellectual and sensory knowledge, and thus to undermine the Platonistic dualism.

8 IDEAS AND SCIENCE

According to the Platonistic interpretation, scientific knowledge

12 FREEDOM AND ACTION

13 THE INNER SELF

Chronological Table

Introduction

Descartes was born into an old, honourable and moderately wealthy French provincial family in 1596. He was brought up as a Catholic and was educated in the newly founded Jesuit college of La Flèche, which he left at the age of eighteen. After a brief military career, and a few years of travel throughout Europe, he decided to seek peace and solitude in Holland. His inherited wealth was sufficient to support him in the style of a respectable gentleman, and he was able to devote himself to research in mathematics, physics, biology and metaphysics. At the end of his life, Queen Christina of Sweden persuaded him to join her court in Stockholm. The necessity of rising early in the cold climate damaged his health, and he died there in 1650.

He took his motto from Ovid: 'To live happily, we must live in seclusion.'[1] He never married, and his only close emotional relationship was with his illegitimate daughter, who died at the age of five. He is reported to have said 'that he had the religion of his nurse, that he lived in it without misgivings, and that he hoped to die in it with equal tranquillity'.[2] He thought that politics ought to be left to 'those whom God has made sovereign over their people, or to whom He gave enough grace and ardour to be prophets'.[3]

Descartes was a new type of intellectual. He was not dogmatic or apologetic; nor was he spiritual and other-worldly. His attitude to his work was businesslike, though he was fanatically confident in the rightness of his ideas. He took advantage of the rising institutions of printing and the book trade in order to address the growing literate public outside the Church and academic bodies, and thus in his own lifetime he became widely known, both as a philosopher and as a physical scientist. But he never produced a work which gave a complete and accurate account of his theories. His main publications were the *Discourse on Method* (1637) and the *Meditations* (1641). The first was written in French, the second in Latin; but both were designed for a large and varied readership. They were very short, their language was engagingly simple, and they were presented as straightforward first-person autobiographical descriptions of their author's personal intellectual adventures, rather than as academic treatises. Their air of honesty and directness is deceptive, however, since they were composed with the greatest care and are misleading as accounts of the development of Descartes's views. But with these books, Descartes succeeded in inserting his ideas into Western thought outside the traditional intellectual institutions; and they have flourished.

[1]

Science and Philosophy

In March 1619, when he was twenty-three, Descartes told a friend that he intended to publish a 'completely new science'. 'The work is infinite . . . incredibly ambitious,' he said.[1] It would enable him to solve almost any problem in geometry. Descartes could hardly believe that such an important task had fallen to him. He even doubted his sanity. But in November he had a dream which convinced him he had been chosen for the task by God,[2] and that he had discovered 'the foundations of an amazing science'.[3]

Descartes's confidence in his 'completely new science' inspired him for the rest of his life. And before long many of his contemporaries came to share it. Ten years later, for instance, he went to a meeting in Paris where a talk was being given by a nobleman called Chandoux. Chandoux was giving expression to the widespread feeling that it was time for science to emancipate itself from the orthodox scholastic Aristotelian philosophy of the Church. Descartes's first biographer, Adrien Baillet, reported that Chandoux's remarks were applauded by everyone at the meeting except Descartes, who claimed that fundamentally they were no better than scholasticism. He proceeded to give an exposition of his own 'novel and infallible method for avoiding sophisms'.

He knew no means more infallible than that which he used himself, a means he had drawn from the foundations of mathematics and by the help of which, he thought, there was no truth he could not demonstrate clearly . . . This method was none other than his 'universal rule', which he also called his 'natural method' . . . There was no one in the room who did not feel the force of his arguments.

One member of the audience was Cardinal Bérulle, who was so impressed by Descartes that he requested a private meeting with him. When Descartes called on Bérulle a few days later, he explained his plan for overthrowing the 'useless methods of scholasticism'. 'He gave glimpses of the consequences these ideas might have, if they were properly developed, and of the practical advantages which might result if this method of philosophising were applied to medicine and mechanics.'[4]

By 1628, then, Descartes thought he was in a position to revolutionize not only geometry, but also the whole of physical science. He thought he had discovered a new method 'for the correct use of reason and for seeking truth in the sciences',[5] and that this would enable him to construct an all-embracing system of scientific theory, including amongst other things medicine, mechanics and mathematics. He would make men into 'masters and possessors of Nature',[6] and he would show that nearly everything that had been taken for science in the past was really nothing but prejudice, superstition and illusion.

Descartes thought that his philosophy would make it possible for scientists to understand the real nature of things, instead of being misled by superficial appearances. Astrology, for instance, was undeniably systematic and sophisticated, but according to Descartes it was unscientific because it was not based on knowledge of the real nature of the stars.[7] But most modern thinkers, although they share Descartes's hostility to astrology, are suspicious of his attempt to base this hostility on philosophical reflections on the natures of things rather than on scientific experiments. They feel that Descartes's philosophical theory of science belongs to the same old-fashioned and obsolete outlook as Descartes wanted to reject.[8]

The source of this uncomprehending attitude to Descartes's theory of science can be called empiricism. Empiricism sees science as independent of philosophy, or at least of philosophy as traditionally conceived. It says that the only legitimate concern of science is with 'matters of fact', which it tends to identify with matters ascertained by the senses, while philosophy, if it has any function at all, is concerned with something different, such as 'matters of logic'. It tends to see the aim of scientific activity as the accumulation of separate bits of information each of which could, in theory if not in practice, be obtained by pure, unprejudiced, passive observation, and without adopting any particular theory or considering the total situation to which they refer.[9] According to empiricism, no philosopher could make the sort of contribution to science which Descartes thought he was making.

The empiricist criticism of Descartes's attempts to rebuild science concentrates on the question of the nature of causal relationships. Empiricists say that a cause and its effect must be two separate things, each of which can be classified or described independently of the other. Descartes, however, seems to have thought the opposite. He wrote: 'We cannot inquire into what an effect is like [*qualis sit effectus*] until we know its cause.'[10] The apparent difference of opinion can be illustrated by reference to attempts to find the cause of rainbows. Descartes, who was himself the first to work out the correct account of the cause of rainbows,[11] would have said that to know what rainbows are like, or to know their nature, is the same as to know their cause. Empiricists reject such statements. G. E. Moore, for example, says: 'It has been too commonly assumed that to show what was the cause of something is the same as to show what the thing itself is. It is, however, hardly necessary to point out that this is not the case.'[12] Such blank refusal to accept Descartes's way of talking about causal relationships, though very common, has no solid basis. It merely grows from ignorance of a very important feature of explanations: the relativity of explanation.

Explanations are relative in the sense that their validity always depends, amongst other things, on how the thing to be explained is described or conceived. For instance, if someone is run over by a bus, his injuries can be thought of in purely biological terms. In this case, his injuries can only be explained in terms of the way his body was damaged when certain parts of it were crushed by a heavy object. Alternatively, the injuries can be thought of as the result of a road accident, and in this case they will have to be explained in terms of things like the carelessness of the bus-driver, or the inefficiency of the brakes on the bus. Similarly, the effect of a cyclone striking a certain place can be thought of in purely meteorological terms, and then it can be explained by reference to various meteorological facts. But the effect can also be thought of in terms of the fact that the cyclone struck an area of Bangladesh which was densely populated and completely unprotected. When it is thought of in this way, the effect can only be explained – if it can be explained at all – by referring to facts of economic and political geography, as well as meteorological facts.

These examples are not sufficient to prove that the empiricist's notion that the nature of an effect can be known independently of its cause is mistaken, but they do show that his conception of cause does not provide him with any good reason for objecting to Descartes's attempt to connect science with philosophy. They show that the way something is explained determines how it should be described, and vice versa; and that to explain something described in one way is not necessarily to explain it described in another way. This implies that the construction of a science involves decisions between various ways of describing things, or of conceiving them. Descartes's philosophy can be seen as, in part, an attempt to discover the most scientific forms of description. This project makes sense however the causal relationship is defined.

Because they ignore the relativity of explanation, empiricists are unable to understand either Descartes or the seventeenth-century scientific revolution as a whole. They think that before the revolution in physical science people were in the grip of unreasonable prejudices which prevented them from realizing that there can be no substitute for the hard work of collecting facts, and they think that the only thing which deserves to be called the philosophy of the revolution in physical science was the destruction of these prejudices. They think that in the seventeenth century the mists of pre-scientific thought lifted to reveal theoretical principles which should have been obvious to people throughout the history of human thought. They see figures like Copernicus (1473–1543), Galileo (1564–1642) and Newton (1642–1727) as pioneers or consolidators of this movement towards enlightenment, but because of Descartes's attempt to base science on philosophy, they tend to think that Descartes had no part in the process.

Galileo, however, saw the new physical science as the result not of a negative retreat from prejudice, but of a tremendous effort of creative thought. He thought that the splendour of Copernicus's achievement in proclaiming that the earth moves around the sun was not that he stated obvious facts which had for some reason been unnoticed in the past, but that, on the contrary, he ignored them:

> I cannot sufficiently admire the eminence of those men's wits, that have received and held it to be true, and with the sprightliness of their own judgements offered such violence to their own senses, as that they have been able to prefer that which their reason dictated to them, to that which sensible experiments represented most manifestly to the contrary . . . I cannot find any bounds for my admiration, how that Reason was able in [men like] . . . Copernicus, to commit such a rape on their senses, as in despite thereof to make herself mistress of their credulity.[13]

Descartes's philosophy was a systematic exploration of the basis and justification for the great intellectual breaks or discontinuities, like those made by Copernicus, on which the seventeenth-century scientific revolution was founded.

All science would be superfluous if the outward appearance and the essence of things directly coincided.

Karl Marx[14]

The most famous work in which Descartes explained his theory of science is the *Discourse on Method*. But although he referred to this elegant essay as a 'project for a universal science'[15] he said that in it he did not 'expound the nature of the method, but only talked about it'.[16] Descartes's fullest explanation of his method is to be found in an earlier work, the *Rules for the Direction of the Mind*, which was written in about

1628, the year he met Chandoux and Bérulle. It was never finished, and it was not published until fifty years after Descartes's death.[17] It is a graceless piece of writing, and at first sight it can seem merely eccentric. It was meant to bring scientific knowledge within the reach of every reader, by summarizing scientific method in a few simple rules. But many of the rules are fussy and obvious; for instance, one of them recommends writing things down in order to 'avoid error due to lapses of memory'.[18] This unpromising exterior, however, encloses fundamental elements of the philosophy of the seventeenth-century scientific revolution.

The most important theme of the *Rules* is reductionism, which is the view that numerous types of things can and should be explained in terms of, or reduced to, a small number of basic features of reality. An example of a reductionist theory is the modern theory that light is a form of electromagnetic radiation, or in other words that it can be analysed as or reduced to electromagnetic radiation. According to Descartes's philosophy of science, the only valid form of explanation was reductionist. The supreme expression of this reductionism was his attempt, in all his extensive writings on physical science, to reduce all physical phenomena to the fundamental properties of physical particles.

In the *Rules*, Descartes expressed his reductionism in terms of the concepts of 'simple natures' and 'composite natures'.[19] The purpose of science, he said, was to reduce composite natures to simple ones.[20] A complete scientific theory would describe the world as a system of natures, showing how all sorts of composite natures can be reduced to simple ones.

Descartes regarded nearly all objects of everyday experience, such as heat, light, magnetism, rainbows, anger, love or the human body, as composite natures. And in the Twelfth Rule he gave some examples of the simple natures to which science should reduce all such things. First there were mental simple natures (*intellectuales*), such as knowledge, doubt, ignorance and will; secondly, physical simple natures, such as shape (*figura*), extension (*extensio*), in other words the property of occupying space, and movement (*motus*); and thirdly, common simple natures, such as existence, unity and duration.[21] The common simple natures were not supposed to be an independent group; they belonged with both the mental and the physical systems of natures.[22] Thus there were, in Descartes's opinion, two basic sets of simple natures, mental and physical ones. This suggests that he thought there were two systems of natures, and so two sciences, mental and physical. In the period when he wrote the *Rules*, Descartes concentrated on the physical natures rather than the mental ones, and he always illustrated his theory of science with examples of how various apparently diverse physical phenomena could be reduced to the same small set of physical simple natures.

It might be said that there was nothing very original in Descartes's reductionism. It is certainly true that before Descartes Francis Bacon (1561-1626) had expressed a similar view; but there is also a case for saying that reductionism is present even in very ancient types of explanation. For example, it seems to be associated with the wide class of explanations that can be called subsumptive explanations. These are explanations which subsume the particular or the specific under general example of this type of explanation is to be found in the categories, or which subsume species under genera. An early *Sophist*, where Plato (427-347) showed how an angler could be explained as a huntsman or, in more general terms, as a practitioner of an art.[23] This method of explanation is called the 'method of division' because it consists essentially in dividing general categories into more specific sub-categories. It was systematized by the neo-Platonist Porphyry (233-305), who constructed what is known as the 'Tree of Porphyry', which is summed up in the diagram overleaf.

The diagram shows how individual things like Socrates and Plato belong to several categories of several degrees of generality where the more general categories include the more specific ones. It is reductionist in the sense that it tries to show that things like Socrates and Plato can be explained in terms of

94902

College of St. Francis Library
Joliet, Illinois

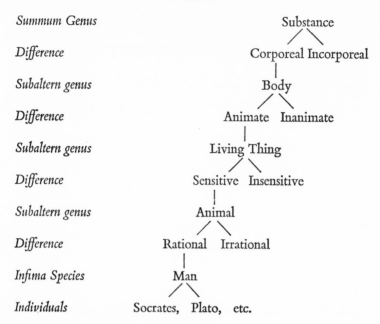

Summum Genus	Substance
Difference	Corporeal Incorporeal
Subaltern genus	Body
Difference	Animate Inanimate
Subaltern genus	Living Thing
Difference	Sensitive Insensitive
Subaltern genus	Animal
Difference	Rational Irrational
Infima Species	Man
Individuals	Socrates, Plato, etc.

things like animality and rationality; it tries to reduce the particular to the general. Various scientific theories, such as the theories that the earth is a sphere, the heart a pump, and light a form of electromagnetic radiation, could be set out in a similar way, and considered as subsumptive explanations, or uses of the method of division.

But there seem to be important differences between the classical method of division and reductionist, scientific theories. The theory that Socrates can be explained in terms of rationality does not seem to be a contribution to scientific knowledge in the way that the theory that light can be explained in terms of electromagnetic radiation does (see below, pp. 40-41, 46-48). In spite of his general contempt for antiquity, however, Descartes saw his own reductionist theory of science as a variation on the method of division as exemplified in the Tree of Porphyry. His objection to Porphyry was that he had selected unscientific categories, and 'division is no good, unless it is of true genera into true species'.[24] Descartes brought philosophy to the aid of physics in order to indicate more scientific ways of describing the world than those which had been used in the past; and his first criticism of old-fashioned approaches was that they were not based on mathematics.

[2]

Mathematics

John Stuart Mill said that Descartes's work in mathematics was 'the greatest single step ever made in the history of the exact sciences'.[1] And according to John Aubrey, Thomas Hobbes 'was wont to say that had Des Cartes kept himselfe wholy to Geometrie that he had been the best Geometer in the world but that his head did not lye for Philosophy.'[2] Descartes shared this high opinion of his mathematics. He said his geometry was 'as superior to ordinary geometry as Cicero's rhetoric is to the child's A B C';[3] and according to one of his friends, 'he said that he had achieved all he could hope for in arithmetic and geometry: that is, he had achieved all that was humanly possible.'[4]

It is widely believed that Descartes's mathematical innovations belong to geometry. In particular, it is often said that his achievement was the creation of co-ordinate geometry, which is a technique for describing curves in terms of algebraic equations. But the importance of Descartes's work in this field has been exaggerated. There were anticipations of it long before the seventeenth century.[5] Descartes himself, who was never reticent about taking credit where he thought it was due, did not attach much importance to co-ordinate geometry.[6] In spite of the fact that his main mathematical treatise was entitled *Geometry*, it was mainly a contribution to what would now be called algebra.[7]

Descartes often used geometrical examples to illustrate what were essentially techniques for solving algebraical problems.[8] He did this because he was convinced that imagination or visualization, and in particular the use of diagrams, had a crucial part to play in scientific investigation. In the *Rules*, for example, he said that even when we study very abstract

28

mathematical questions 'we ought to imagine something, and use the intellect not on its own but helped by images formed in the imagination [*speciebus in fantasia depictis*] . . . It will be a great help if we apply whatever people say about magnitudes in general, to that species of magnitudes which can be pictured easiest in the imagination.'[9] He even went so far as to say, 'We refuse to countenance philosophical entities, which cannot literally be imagined [*quae revera sub imaginationem non cadunt*].'[10] And he suggested that mathematicians are bound to make mistakes if they suppose that geometry is not about real, physical things.[11]

In the *Discourse* he was more specific, saying that in dealing with mathematical problems it was always best to think of the magnitudes involved 'as having the form of straight lines'.[12] But he also warned against 'fatiguing the imagination' by using diagrams to deal with really complicated problems. It was better to use algebra instead. In this way, he concluded, the scientist would be 'taking the best from geometrical analysis and algebra, each making up for the deficiencies of the other'.[13]

The full importance of Descartes's work in mathematics can only be appreciated when it is remembered that in Descartes's time the understanding of mathematical operations was crude and unsophisticated. In particular, mathematicians were puzzled about operations like squaring and cubing a number.

He [Descartes] was so eminently learned that all learned men made visits to him, and many of them would desire him to shew them his instruments (in those dayes mathematicall learning lay much in the knowledge of Instruments, and, as Sir Henry Savile sayd, in doeing of tricks) he would drawe out a little Drawer under his Table, and shew them a paire of Compasses with one of the Legges broken; and then, for his Ruler, a sheet of paper folded double.

John Aubrey[14]

For one thing, they were hindered by inadequate symbolism. As Descartes said, algebraical knowledge was crippled by the 'complicated numbers and incomprehensible shapes [*figuras*]' in which it was expressed.[15] He himself invented the modern notation, which uses small numerals to represent exponents, for example putting x^2 for x squared.

But the difficulties were not simply a matter of notation. Mathematicians were not at all clear about what the real meaning of operations like cubing and squaring was. They tended to think of such operations in a crudely spatial way, in terms of areas and volumes (squares and cubes); and this made the use of exponents greater than three almost completely unintelligible to them. Stevinus (1548–1640) had suggested thinking of the use of such exponents in terms of cubes being placed on top of one another.[16] And Descartes once suggested, in a similar vein, that they should be thought of in terms of cubes made of various materials – a wooden cube representing the third power, a stone cube the fourth, an iron one the fifth, and so on.[17]

The discovery which made Descartes claim in 1628 that he had achieved 'all that was humanly possible' in geometry and arithmetic was of a 'general algebra' which used 'not the shapes of bodies but plane (i.e. two-dimensional) ones, as these are more readily understood'.[18] The plane diagrams Descartes used consisted of dots, straight lines and rectangles, and were far less clear and elegant than the curves co-ordinated with straight lines which he was to use in the *Geometry*,[19] and which have led him to be credited with the discovery of co-ordinate geometry. Their importance is that they enabled squaring, cubing and so on to be conceived of in non-spatial terms, and thus expanded the range of algebra, and prepared the way for the sophisticated use of exponents other than positive whole numbers, which was to play a central part in later developments in mathematics.[20]

Up to Descartes's time, certain types of curves had been described as 'mechanical' as opposed to 'geometrical', because it was thought that although they could be drawn mechanically, in several unrelated movements, they could not be described geometrically or mathematically. The discovery from which Descartes's confidence in his scientific genius derives – the discovery of which he boasted extravagantly in March 1619 – was that certain of these curves had a perfect right to be regarded as geometrical rather than mechanical. Oddly enough, his belief in the importance of graphic illustration of abstract mathematical facts made him express his discovery that these curves were not mechanical by describing a special machine or instrument, a sort of pair of compasses, which could be used to draw them. The fact that the curves in question could be generated by a single movement of these compasses showed that they ought to be regarded as geometrical, because it meant that they corresponded to precise and soluble mathematical equations.[21]

But Descartes did not dispose of the notion of mechanical lines altogether. He still thought that certain types of curves were 'mechanical', in the sense that they could not be described mathematically.[22] It was left to a later generation of mathematicians, and in particular to Leibniz (1646–1716), to say that mathematics was capable of dealing with any curve whatever. Leibniz renamed Descartes's 'mechanical' lines 'transcendental' – a usage that still survives – and said that these 'must be received into geometry, whatever M. Descartes may say'.[23]

Descartes's success in extending the limits of mathematical science to include problems which had formerly been relegated to mechanics provided an inspiring example of the improvement of human knowledge.[24] But Descartes saw it as more than an example: according to him, mathematics was the very essence of science, and in particular of physics. 'True physics,' he wrote, 'is a branch of mathematics . . . It is through mathematics alone that knowledge of true physics can be attained.'[25] His whole theory of science was based on his 'true', 'abstract' or 'universal' mathematics.[26] His method, he said in the *Discourse on Method*, was distilled from logic, geometrical analysis and algebra. It took 'all that is best in these disciplines, while remaining free of their defects'.[27] The *Discourse* was written as a preface to three scientific papers by Descartes, which were supposed to be 'essays in the Method'. [28] One of these was the *Geometry*. Another was the *Dioptrics*, which is about vision, the nervous system and light, and which reports Descartes's discovery of the sine-law of refraction.[29] The third was the *Meteors*, which is about subjects like rain and lightning, and contains Descartes's explanation of rainbows. Descartes thought that the *Dioptrics* and the *Meteors* would be useful for persuading people that his method was 'superior to the common one'. 'But,' he added, 'I pride myself on having demonstrated it in the *Geometry*.'[30]

Descartes's recommendation that science should be based on geometry is often interpreted as implying that scientific theories should be expounded in the style known as the 'geometrical method of exposition', which sets out theories by beginning with numbered definitions, axioms and postulates, and then deduces lemmas, corollaries and theorems from them. But this interpretation is completely wrong. Descartes said explicitly that the geometrical method was useless in physics,[31] and he hardly ever used it himself.[32] There is no trace of it in his *Geometry*.

This misunderstanding of the connection between Descartes's method and geometry is often used as a basis for criticizing Descartes's theory of science. He is said to have tried to apply types of reasoning suitable only in mathematics and philosophy to a field which is neither mathematical nor philosophical, namely physics.[33] Contrary to what these critics assume, however, scientific theories can perfectly well be expressed by the 'geometrical method', and it would not have mattered at all if Descartes had favoured it. In fact any theory, regardless of its structure and subject matter, can be expressed by it.[34] Leibniz once cast a piece of political propaganda in the 'geometrical' form.[35]

Descartes's insistence that physics is a branch of mathematics was far more sensible and significant than his critics have realized. The first of the two main points about it was that it led to an extremely important restriction on what sorts of things could be simple and composite natures, and hence on what sorts of things could be the subject-matter of science. This is that the simple natures must be capable of being treated mathematically, and hence that they must be quantities. (Descartes apparently applied this restriction to the physical system of natures, rather than the mental one.) Descartes's 'universal mathematics' dealt only with problems 'in which order and measure are to be examined'.[36] So as a branch of mathematics, physical science had to limit itself to the measurable aspects of things – to their 'dimensions', as Descartes called them – such as length, breadth and depth, and also weight (*gravitas*) which is 'the dimension of a thing's heaviness' and speed which is 'the dimension of movement'.[37] Other aspects of physical things, such as their colour and smell, would be ignored by physics if they could not be explained in terms of, or reduced to, 'dimensions'. The language of physics would have to be purely mathematical.

The second main connection between Descartes's physics and his 'universal mathematics' derives from the fact that his mathematical techniques were based on labelling each quantity (or 'dimension') in a problem, whether known or unknown, with a special symbol.[38] This practice had been originated by Vieta (1540–1623) in 1594, and had been improved by Descartes when he introduced the convention, still in use today, of using lower-case letters from the beginning of the alphabet to stand for known quantities, and ones from the end to stand for unknowns.[39]

In the *Rules*, Descartes explained the advantages of labelling all the variables in a problem. He took an application of Pythagoras's theorem as an example.

If you want to know the hypotenuse of a right-angle triangle, given that the other two sides measure 9 and 12, an arithmetician (*logista*) will tell you it is $\sqrt{225}$, that is, 15. We, however, instead of putting '9' and '12' will put '*a*' and '*b*', and will discover that the hypotenuse is $\sqrt{a^2+b^2}$. Thus we will keep these two parts – a^2 and b^2 – which would otherwise be confused in the number – distinct ... We have to make these distinctions if we are to get a distinct and evident knowledge (*cognitionem evidentam et distinctam*) of things, The arithmeticians, however, are happy if they get the right answer. without understanding properly how it depends on the known quantities: all the same, it is in this that true science consists.[40]

In other words, the technique enabled one to keep track of the basic known quantities in a problem even when they were subjected to complex operations.[41] Scientific knowledge would be the product of seeing things in terms of the contributions which the simple natures make to them, and in keeping these 'distinct', where they would otherwise be 'confused'. Ordinary sensory experience tended to lead to this sort of confusion. In order to sort it out a new and critical approach to the facts of experience was required.

[3]

Method

Descartes's theory of science set up the ideal of reducing all sorts of phenomena to a few basic variables. His account of scientific method was an attempt to describe the steps a scientist would have to take in order to realize this ideal. It explained how one should set about criticizing the conceptions on which common sense and traditional physical theory were based, and replacing them with genuinely scientific ones.

At one level, Descartes's method was quite simple. He advised the investigator to try to get a wide and varied experience of his subject, while constantly trying to think of it as reducible to a few basic variables – the simple natures. In the *Rules*, he spelt out how this method might be used by someone who wanted to investigate magnetism.

> The person who realises that there can be nothing to know in the magnet which does not consist of certain self-evident (*per se notis*) simple natures, will know exactly how to proceed. First he will collect all the experiences he can get of the stone. From these he will try to deduce the character of the intermixture of simple natures which is necessary to produce the effects he has experienced in connection with the magnet. When he has done this, he will be able to claim with confidence that he has discovered the true nature of the magnet, insofar as knowledge can be derived from these experiences ... We will get as far as the limits of the human mind allow if we see very distinctly (*distinctissime*) the mixture of familiar things or natures (*jam notorum entium sive naturarum mixturam*) which would produce the observed effect in the magnet.[1]

Descartes's conception of how this sort of investigation should proceed was modelled on algebra. An observed composite nature, such as magnetism, corresponded to variables representing known quantities, and the combination of simple natures to which it was to be reduced corresponded to a set of variables whose value was unknown. The values of the variables representing the simple natures would be discovered by observing what values the others had in the widest possible range of situations. The resulting sets of equations would then be solved by techniques which are explained in the *Geometry*;[2] and one would have achieved the scientific ideal of showing how the observed phenomena could be completely accounted for in terms of a small set of basic quantities, the simple natures.

Descartes referred to this method of investigation as the analytic method. A primitive version of the analytic method was known to ancient Greek geometers, and had been taken over by Plato. For Plato, it meant the 'method of hypothesis', which consists in working out the implications of the hypothesis that a thing has a certain nature, or that a variable has a certain value, without committing oneself to saying that the hypothesis in question is true.[3] Descartes seems not to have realized how crude this notion of analysis was. He was puzzled by the fact that ancient mathematicians had not pointed out how it could be applied to science, and so arrived at his method. The only explanation he could think of was that 'they attached such importance to it that they kept it to themselves as an important secret'.[4] But in fact it was only with sixteenth- and seventeenth-century developments in algebra, and in particular with the invention of the technique of labelling all the variables in a problem, whether known or unknown, that the notion of analysis had come to have any obvious bearing on questions of scientific method. After these advances, analysis could be identified with the technique of naming all the variables and trying to evaluate the unknown ones by forming equations, and it was easy for thinkers like Galileo, Newton and Leibniz to see that analysis, understood in this sense, could cast light on problems of reductive science.[5]

In the *Rules*, Descartes explained the analytic method by saying that the investigation of scientific questions ought to be governed by the search for absolutes as opposed to relatives.[6] The term 'relatives' applied to two rather different classes of things. First, it applied to those aspects of a scientific problem which seemed likely to be completely inexplicable. Descartes called these *respectus*. It seems likely that he thought of them as corresponding to the 'mechanical' curves which, in his opinion,

---

The beginning of an acquaintance, whether with persons or things, is to get a definite outline for our ignorance.

George Eliot[7]

---

could not be explained mathematically. Descartes did not give any examples of *respectus*, but he probably had in mind things like colours as conceived by common sense. Before stating his reductionist theory of light, Descartes warned that his theory might not explain colours, as people normally think of them. 'There may be a difference,' he said, 'between the sensation (*sentiment*) we have of it (i.e. of light) . . . and that in the object which causes the sensation in us.'[8] His theory of light was meant to explain the physical nature of light, rather than the facts of visual experience.

The second class of things which Descartes referred to as 'relative' were ones which were so complicated or freakish that they were a very unpromising starting-point for a scientific investigation, even though it might be hoped that they would eventually be explained. 'The reason for this is that such rarities are often misleading, as long as one remains ignorant of the causes of more everyday things; and that the conditions they depend on are nearly always so peculiar and minute as to be very difficult to discover.'[9] The purpose of concentrating on absolutes and ignoring relatives was to make it easy to identify the simple natures. In the Sixth Rule Descartes listed a number of criteria which he thought would be helpful for separating absolutes from relatives. The absolutes, he said, were whatever is independent, a cause, simple, universal, one (as opposed to multiple), equal, similar, straight (as opposed to curved) and so on.[10]

These suggestions have baffled many readers. But given the importance of algebraical techniques in Descartes's approach to problems of scientific method, most of them are fairly easy to understand. One needs to form equations – hence *equality*. And one needs equations which involve the simple natures, which operate as *causes* rather than effects and which are in this sense *independent*. One should avoid *multiplicity* in order to arrive at equations which are not too complicated to solve. The equations one uses should be as *simple* as possible,[11] corresponding to *straight* lines rather than curves.[12] And since the object of the investigation is to give unified explanations of diverse phenomena – for example heat and light[13] – one should try to bring out their fundamental *similarity*.[14]

Descartes also said that the absolutes are *universal*, and this requirement too has confused many people. In medieval philosophy the word 'universal' was used in discussing what gives general terms, like 'table', their ability to stand for an indefinite number of particular individuals. In the context of this discussion, universals tended to be thought of, both by their advocates and by their enemies, as abstract or ideal objects, such as 'tableness', which were somehow present in and common to all the individuals to which the general term applied. Descartes, with most other thinkers of his time, was impatient with this discussion, and said that he refused to acknowledge such things, or at least that they ought to be thought of as mere 'modes of thought'.[15]

Obviously Descartes was not using the word 'universal' in this medieval sense when he said that the absolutes were universal. The context makes it clear that he was using the word in the sense it has in phrases like 'universal suffrage' and 'universal gravitation',[16] so his meaning was that the absolutes were ubiquitous or completely general, which implied that scientific inquiry ought to concentrate on ubiquitous phenomena. The reason for this advice was that the simple natures to which everything explicable would be reduced by a fully developed physical science, were themselves ubiquitous. These simple natures were features of every particle in the universe.

Descartes's universality requirement expresses his disagreement with Francis Bacon's view that science could only advance by accumulating detailed records of all sorts of unusual occurrences. Bacon had said: 'We have to make a collection or particular natural history of all prodigies and monstrous births of nature; of everything in short that is in nature new, rare, and unusual.'[17] Descartes commented: 'I have nothing to add to what Bacon has written, except that it does not do to be over-curious about discovering the details [*particularités*] of a subject: the important thing is to make general surveys of the most common things.'[18] He amplified this comment in the *Discourse*: 'To begin with it is best to make use of those [observations] which immediately present themselves to the senses – of which we cannot be ignorant, however little we attend to them – rather than of those which are rare and esoteric.'[19] Descartes thought that both Galileo[20] and the mathematician Fermat[21] had failed to take note of this point. Perhaps his criticisms of these two scientists were unjustified: there can be no doubt that they were inspired partly by jealousy. But if he had lived to hear the amazing stories which passed for contributions to science in the later days of the Royal Society – such as stories of 'Horny Girles', of a man of Prague who ate a whole live hog with the bristles on, and of a headless child who lived for four days, thus proving that the soul is not located in the head – he would have insisted on his point still more emphatically, and with more obvious justification.

Descartes did not give much space to explicit discussion of the universality requirement; but it represents one of his most decisive breaks with past theories of science and one of the most important philosophical features of the seventeenth-century scientific revolution. The physicists of the past had incorporated certain qualitative distinctions, which were deeply engrained in ordinary ways of experiencing the world, into the foundations of physical theory. For example, they had thought that some things had the fundamental property of being in motion, while others did not, that some things had the fundamental property of being hot, while others did not, and so on. They did not try to explain such properties in terms of more basic and universal ones. Descartes's universality requirement, however, implied that references to such irreducible, non-universal properties ought to be expelled from basic scientific theory. According to Descartes, science should explain everything in terms of universal properties. It followed that things like heat and motion needed to be conceptualized in a new way or else not be referred to at all. They had to be defined in terms of scalar quantities or 'dimensions', which were universal in the sense of being possessed in some degree by every particle in the universe, rather than as irreducible properties which some things had and others did not. Even stationary things should be considered as being in a certain state of motion, namely a zero state of motion; and even cold things should be considered as having a certain degree of heat or temperature.

The universality requirement had very definite implications for scientific theories and had a profound influence on their development. For example, it was used against Galileo, who thought that different things moved in irreducibly different ways. According to Galileo, 'violent' and 'natural' motions, and motions in a circle and motions in a straight line, could not be explained by a unified and universal theory of motion.[22] In spite of Galileo's importance in the development of the theory of motion, the development could not make further progress until it had discarded these views of his. The universality requirement also contributed to the development of chemical theory, because it implied that a chemical analysis was not complete when it had reached the Aristotelian 'elements' of earth, air, fire and water, or the chemical 'principles' of salt, sulphur and mercury: it would only be complete when these elements or principles were themselves explained in terms of properties common to every particle in the universe.

It is now possible to see one reason why the ancient method of division, which has results like the definition of man as a rational animal, seems feeble and unscientific compared with modern reductive explanations (see above, p.26). The reductive classifications which Descartes saw at the heart of science, being framed in terms of universal, quantitative properties, were capable of having a completely different structure from ancient species-genus classifications like the Tree of Porphyry.

The ancient classifications took a single supremely general category and divided it over and over again until they reached 'basic species'. Hence their 'tree' structure: the general category was the trunk and the 'basic species' were the tips of the branches. Such classifications are somewhat uninformative because they do not give any explanation of why the general categories should be divided in the way they are. For example, they do not explain why the class of animals should be divided into two species, rational and irrational. For this reason, according to Descartes, the Tree of Porphyry was useless; it would 'drag us into a maze from which we could never escape', and end up 'in pure tautology, which would clarify nothing, and leave us in our original ignorance'.[23]

... So we certainly cannot hope to learn about Nature by means of vague and arbitrary hypotheses; we can only do it by the critical study of phenomena, by the comparisons we shall make between them, by the art of reducing, as far as possible, a large number of phenomena to a single one which can be regarded as fundamental.

d'Alembert[24]

The sorts of classifications which Descartes recommended had a different structure. They were like a tree with several trunks, for they were based on several basic categories (corresponding to the simple natures), rather than on one supremely general category. Every physical phenomenon, if it was capable of being explained scientifically, could be completely described in terms of the same basic categories; and all these basic categories applied to all physical phenomena. The basic categories were not divided on principles which were external to them; instead, they were 'diversified by one another'.[25] All sorts of physical things – rainbows, magnets, stars, plants, animals and human bodies – would be classified in terms of the same small set of universal dimensions.

Descartes's treatment of the old-fashioned concepts of

scholastic Aristotelianism was extremely unfair and inaccurate.[26] This is particularly true of his rejection of 'final cause' or
'teleological' explanations.[27] As Aristotle saw it, the final cause
of something was its aim or purpose (*telos*). In this sense
breathing is the final cause of lungs; its attraction for bees is the
final cause of the scent of flowers; and, it might be argued, the
creation of surplus value is the final cause of capitalism.
Descartes, however, assumed that the only things which could
have aims or purposes were things which could think, and so
he thought that teleological explanations only applied to the
products of such beings.[28] He concluded that their application
to anything else involved a confusion of the mental and the
physical, and was nothing but a relic of the primitive magic
which sees purely physical phenomena as the operations of
thinking beings. But, in fact, as the examples of lungs, capitalism and the scent of flowers show, Descartes's assumption
was unjustified, or at least stood in need of somest renuous
argumentation. The examples suggest that final-cause explanations can be used wherever there is a system whose parts are
governed by the system as a whole. It seems that Descartes
simply ignored the possibility of such systems.

The confusion of final-cause explanations with explanations
in terms of thought was common at the time of the revolution
in physical science. It can be found for instance in the works of
Francis Bacon. In fact a great deal of Descartes's criticism of
Aristotelian concepts and jargon, of 'occult properties' and
'substantial forms', seems merely to echo the exhilarating
rallying-cries of the iconoclastic anti-Aristotelian movement
which had begun in the Renaissance.[29] But unlike most of the
other anti-Aristotelians, Descartes came very close to providing
a positive alternative to Aristotelianism. The Aristotelian view
was that specific phenomena should be explained in terms of
their specific and irreducible natures or essences, rather than in
universal terms. The phrases 'substantial form' and 'occult
property' simply meant these irreducible, specific properties.[30]
He did this by giving a clear and well-worked-out statement of
the scientific ideal of explaining everything in terms of a few

universal, quantitative properties, 'namely the shape, size, arrangement and motion of material particles'. He proclaimed that 'there are no occult forces in stones or plants, none of these stupendous and miraculous sympathies and antipathies, in fact that nothing in the whole universe (*in natura universa*) need be referred to anything but purely physical causes – i.e. ones completely independent of mind and thought.'[31]

Empiricist thinkers tend to think that the main effect of the revolution in physical science was the rise of the habit of making systematic observations and experiments, the creation of institutions to promote this and the use of the knowledge so acquired to extend human control over nature. As they see it, the culmination of the seventeenth-century scientific revolution is the work of modern university and industrial laboratories. At least in theory, Descartes acknowledged the importance of observation and experiment. He appealed on several occasions for financial assistance with programmes of scientific research,[32] and one of his reasons for publishing the *Discourse on Method* was the hope of getting help with the 'infinite number of observations (*expériences*)' required to complete his scientific work.[33] He also pioneered certain experimental techniques, especially in optics and vivisection.[34] But he did not think that the essence of science was experimental work. Indeed, he did not think of science as a cumulative activity which could last for generations and generations; he thought that within a few years he or his immediate followers would have worked out a complete and unimprovable system of scientific knowledge. And most of his scientific works were written at a level of abstraction which gives them a flavour very different from that of the works of other great seventeenth-century scientists.[35] He tended to be impatient with the practical details of experimentation, and to make rash anticipations or unjustified interpretations of the results.[36] It is true that the same might be said of other great scientists, even Newton;[37] but Descartes's attitude to organized experiment and observation was undeniably quite exceptionally careless.

The seventeenth-century scientific revolution involved not only the rise of organized science, but also the rise of the mechanical philosophy. Without its philosophical dimension, the rise of organized science would not have been a scientific revolution. This is proved by the history of astronomy. Astronomy was a highly developed and organized observational science long before the scientific revolution. It did not have much to say about the physical nature of the stars and planets, but it was able to make accurate predictions, based on sophisticated mathematical calculations, of when and where stars would be seen in the sky. Thus Aristotelianism and scholasticism were not incompatible with organized observation and experiment. There were observations which were incompatible with the traditional theories. But such observations had been known long before the seventeenth century,[38] and it took more than the work of patient experimenters to overthrow the old world picture. First it was necessary to create a radically new way of considering the nature of the physical world, and no individual contributed more to this than Descartes. The influence of his reductive ideal on the development of science has been so enormous that it justifies even his most boastful claims about the importance of his work. Newton took over Descartes's belief that the purpose of science was to reduce everything to the 'universal qualities of all bodies whatsoever'.[39] And it was in the spirit of Descartes that he wrote dismissively of the things to which 'the Aristotelians gave the Name of occult Qualities': 'Such occult Qualities put a stop to the Improvement of natural Philosophy, and therefore of late Years have been rejected. To tell us that every Species of Things is endow'd with an occult specifick Quality by which it acts and produces manifest Effects, is to tell us nothing.'[40] Similarly, in advocating the 'investigation of things by the Method of Analysis' he echoes Descartes in speaking of it as moving 'from particular Causes to more general ones, till the Argument end in the most general'.[41] The views of Robert Boyle (1627–91), the central figure in the early days of the Royal Society, were equally close to those of

Descartes. The purpose of his *Origins of Forms and Qualities*, for example, was to show in detail how

almost all sorts of qualities, most of which have been by the schools left unexplicated, or generally referred to I know not what incomprehensible substantial forms, may be produced mechanically; I mean by such corporeal agents, as do not appear to work otherwise, than by virtue of the size, figure, and contrivance of their own parts (which attributes I call the mechanical affections of matter, because to them men willingly refer the various operations of mechanical engines).[42]

The 'mechanical philosophy', as it came to be known, and in particular classical or Newtonian physics, was the realization of Descartes's ideal of a reductive science. Its method was Descartes's.

[4]

Physics

In 1630 Descartes was a young intellectual living an isolated life in the Netherlands. He had not published anything and he had no students. But he was already famous as a physicist, and in at least one college Cartesian physical theory was being taught.[1] By 1632 he had prepared for publication a book on physics, in French, called *The World*. Amongst other things, this book came out in support of the Copernican view that the earth moves around the sun. But in the same year, Galileo was censured by the Roman Church for saying that the earth moved, and Descartes, fearing public controversy, decided to suppress his book. In 1637 he published the *Discourse on Method*, also in French, which contained a brief summary of *The World*. This had an immediate success, especially in England and the Netherlands. In response to increasing demand, Descartes eventually rewrote *The World*, playing down its Copernicanism, and expanding it into a Latin textbook on philosophy and physics for use in colleges. This work, the *Principles of Philosophy*, was published in 1644. But other textbooks of Cartesian physics soon became available, and the *Principles* never became very popular.

Cartesian physics offered what seemed to be a completely new type of scientific explanation. Whereas traditional systems of scientific explanations had been based on abstract categories like animality and rationality, the Cartesian system promised to explain physical phenomena in far more concrete terms – 'without needing to postulate anything in matter other than the movement, size, shape and arrangement of its parts'.[2] Where traditional systems seemed to explain things only by classifying them into specific categories, the Cartesian system seemed to explain things in terms of the stuff they were composed of. That is, in place of the merely subsumptive explanations which had satisfied most scientists in the past, it seemed to offer what can be called compositional explanations. Compositional explanations explain things in terms of their constituents or components. One would be giving a compositional explanation, for example, if one explained the properties of brine in terms of those of salt and water. Such explanations involve the idea that a cause (such as salt) gets used up in the process of producing its effect (in this case, brine). The use of compositional explanations is very widespread. St Mark exploited it in suggesting that when a woman cured herself of illness by touching Jesus's clothes, Jesus could feel 'that the virtue had gone out of him'.[3] Galileo relied on it when he argued that heavenly bodies could not cause 'generation and alteration' on earth unless they underwent changes themselves.[4] And certain psychologists assume the same when they think of drives like aggression as dissipating themselves when they cause behaviour.

There are obviously limits to the possibilities of interpreting explanations as compositional. These limits are dictated by the fact that compositional explanations have to be in terms of things that are substantial. Substantiality, as I understand it here, is a matter of degree. A thing is substantial to the extent that the quantity of it tends to be conserved.[5] Something which is subject to a rigid conservation principle is very substantial indeed; whereas things which can pass out of the world without leaving a trace are very insubstantial. It always makes sense to ask in relation to something substantial, 'where did it come from?' or 'where has it gone?' Smoke is more substantial than flames, and wood is more substantial than smoke. Colours and smells are not substantial at all. Substantial things cannot simply pass out of existence and it is only substantial things which can be regarded as constituents of things. For instance, when a man dies the body which was his, which is substantial, continues to exist in some form or other; but his knowledge of mathematics and his bad health, which are insubstantial, simply cease to exist. The sort of abstractions which the Tree of Porphyry refers to – such as animality and rationality – seem to be very insubstantial. They do not seem to be the kinds of things which could be constituents of men in the way that salt and water are constituents of brine, and they are therefore incapable of figuring in compositional explanations.

Descartes sometimes spoke as though the simple natures were substantial, saying that they 'run together to compose other things' and using phrases like 'intermixture of simple natures'. However, he also said that in one sense at least a physical thing 'cannot be said to be composed of the natures of body, size and shape, since these elements have never existed separately (*distinctae*) from each other'. The only sense in which we could 'call it something composed of these three natures' was one which simply implied that 'we thought of each of them separately before we could judge that they were all found in one and the same subject'.[6]

Descartes's hesitation about regarding his explanations as compositional is understandable. Some at least of the simple natures seem not to be sufficiently substantial to be a basis for compositional explanations. For instance, shape seems insubstantial: when the shapes formed by the frost on my window are melted by the morning sun, they do not go anywhere; they simply disappear. Descartes's other examples of simple natures – the mental ones, like doubt and knowledge, and the common ones, like existence and duration – are perhaps even less substantial; but when he developed his theory of science he paid very little attention to these anyway. This left him with two physical simple natures which might be regarded as substantial, and taken as a basis for compositional explanations. These are size or extension, the dimension of matter; and speed or velocity, the dimension of motion. Matter and motion could be seen as constituting physical things as salt and water constitute brine.[7] 'Give me matter and motion,' he seemed to say, 'and I will make a world.'[8]

In *The World*, Descartes put forward a new concept of motion. 'The virtue or power of moving itself which one discovers in a body can pass in its entirety, or in part, into another, and thus no longer be in the first; but it cannot cease to be in the world altogether.'⁹ Descartes defined this substantial concept of motion more closely in his three 'laws of nature', which are basically conservation principles.¹⁰ They are listed, in different orders, in both *The World* and the *Principles*. Here is the list from *The World*:

(Law One) Every particular body remains in the same state, as long as it is not forced to move by meeting with other bodies (cf. Law One in the *Principles*).
... No one would deny that this applies ... regarding size, shape, rest, and a thousand similar things; but Philosophers have made an exception of movement which is, however, what I would most particularly wish to include.¹¹

The next law simply gave a more quantitative form to the first:

(Law Two) When one body pushes another, it simultaneously loses as much motion as it imparts (cf. Law Three in the *Principles*).¹²

The next law amplified this into the most distinctive and fruitful principle of classical physics: the principle which has since come to be known as the principle of inertia. This states that what is conserved is movement in a straight line.

(Law Three) When a body is moving, even though it will usually be taking a curved path ... nevertheless each particular bit of the body has a tendency to continue its motion in a straight line (cf. Law Two in the *Principles*).¹³

Galileo had propounded something similar to this statement, but said that it only applied to horizontal motions.¹⁴ In removing the restrictions, and making the principle of inertia completely universal, Descartes was laying one of the foundation-stones of classical physics.¹⁵

The physical theory of *The World* can be thought of as an elaboration of the idea that motion is substantial, or that it is an actual constituent of moving things, so that all sorts of physical phenomena could be seen as consisting of different mixtures of matter and motion. However, Descartes never said in so many words that motion was substantial or a constituent of moving things. There were good reasons for this. For one thing, if motion were a sort of substance, which can flow from one thing to another, it would make sense to say that motion itself, as opposed to moving things, can move, and that it might exist without matter. Perhaps Descartes also thought that treating motion as substantial would commit him to the idea that the motion something has, like the salt in a sample of brine, is absolute, or that, without relying on any particular frame of reference (or set of frames) one could say absolutely that some things have motion and others do not. This would imply that a statement like 'the earth moves' is complete in itself and does not need to be supplemented with a phrase like 'relative to the stars'; in other words that space and time are absolute and not relative.

In his later book, the *Principles*, Descartes insisted that motion, like shape, size and arrangement, is only a 'mode' of matter: it was, he said, 'a mode of the moving thing' and 'not a substance'.[16] While tacitly admitting that this made the law of the conservation of motion less obvious[17] he emphasized that 'motion, as a mode of body, cannot pass from one body to another'.[18] The *Principles*, unlike *The World*, contains a completely relativistic account of motion: 'Movement properly understood may be said to relate only to bodies that are contiguous to that in motion.'[19] One reason (perhaps the only reason) why Descartes opted for this relativistic definition of motion was that it enabled him to dissociate himself from the Copernican theory that the earth moves, which he had committed himself to in *The World*, but for which Galileo had been censured by the Church. On the relativistic definition, the earth could not be said to move, since it was surrounded by its atmosphere, in relation to which it was stationary. But the definition was a bad one. As Newton pointed out, it implied that particles on the surface of a moving body move while those inside do not. Newton therefore retained something more like Descartes's early, substantial concept of motion, and felt that this committed him to the notions of absolute motion, absolute space and absolute time.[20] But behind this somewhat baffling disagreement about absolute and relative motion, there was agreement on a far more fundamental point: that motion in a straight line is always conserved.

Descartes constructed not only a new concept of motion, but also a new concept of matter, or 'material substance' as he called it. Matter had traditionally been regarded by philosophers as something quite abstract, a 'pure potentiality'. In itself, it was completely propertiless: it was what underlay essential properties. Descartes rejected this conception of matter: 'I conceive its extension, or the property it has of occupying space, not at all as an accident, but as its true form and essence.'[21]

Thus material substance, according to Descartes, did not *underlie* extension; it was *identical* with extension. In saying this, Descartes was rejecting not only the philosophical view of matter as 'pure potentiality', but also the common-sense view of matter as consisting of solid impenetrable particles moving in space. He thought that the alleged difference between matter and space was really a difference between various forms of material substance.[22] The idea of a vacuum, that is of space without matter, was, he thought, as illusory as those of occult properties and substantial forms: matter and space were identical, and there could be no such thing as a vacuum.

Descartes never put forward much argument for his denial of vacuum. His position is usually summarized by saying that he thought 'nothing can have no properties'. But this paraphrase makes Descartes's argument sound like a mere verbal trick, whereas in fact it involves something important: the conviction that action at a distance is impossible, and that the only way in which one physical thing can affect the movements of another is by having physical contact with it, if only through the intervention of some otherwise undetectable medium. Descartes evidently thought this point too obvious to be worth stating. He assumed that any denial of it would be non-mechanistic and would involve an illegitimate reference to final causes. And in spite of the fact that it is contradicted both by the Newtonian concept of force, and by much modern physical theory, few people would deny that it still has a certain attraction. But it may be doubted whether it proves Descartes's point: it only implies that when one physical thing acts on another there must be matter between them; it does not imply that the whole of space must be filled with matter.

Descartes's reasons for his denial of vacuum were very abstract and hard to grapple with. Contemporaries like Pascal and Gassendi thought they had an experimental refutation of Descartes's position in the fact that an apparently empty space was formed at the top of the column of mercury in a barometer. But Descartes rightly thought that such evidence was inconclusive. There was no better reason for saying that there was a pure vacuum above the mercury, than for saying, as Descartes would, that there was undetected material substance there. And the fact that the so-called vacuum had properties, in particular that it was able to act as a medium for the transmission of light and radiant heat, could be interpreted as experimental proof that there was matter there. When Descartes's opponents confronted his denial of vacuum not with experiments but at its own abstract level, the discussion degenerated into a purely verbal one about whether to talk about a peculiar form of matter or whether to talk about a vacuum instead.[23]

Descartes's denial of vacuum had wide-ranging consequences for his physical theory. It implied that the universe was completely full, and this in turn implied that 'every movement in the world is in a way circular; that is, when a body leaves its position, it immediately takes over the position of another body, and this one that of another, and so on to the last, which immediately occupies the position vacated by the first.'[24] Descartes explained this instantaneous swapping of places by comparing it with fish displacing water while swimming round a pond, and with a turning wheel.[25] One advantage of the theory that any movement involves the movement of a complete ring of particles was that it made it possible to explain various phenomena associated with so-called vacuums, without bringing in any non-mechanistic notions or the notion of action at a distance. Descartes's example was the fact that one has to make a hole in the top of a barrel, to let the air in, before one can get any wine out of the tap. The traditional way of explaining this sort of thing was based on the idea of nature's 'horror' of vacuum. Descartes thought that such explanations were obviously preposterous: 'We know very well that the wine has no mind (*esprit*) to fear things; and even if it had, I cannot imagine why it should be frightened of a vacuum – which after all is a mere chimera.' According to Descartes, the real reason why there had to be a hole in the top of the barrel was simply that 'the portion of air whose place it (the wine) would occupy if it did come out would have nowhere else to go in the whole universe'.[26]

Descartes's theory that all motions are 'in a way circular' also provided most of the materials necessary for the great synthesis which is the heart of classical physics: the use of a physical theory of motion to support the otherwise free-floating Copernican hypothesis that the planets go round the sun, and the explanation of celestial motions on the same principles as motions on earth. Descartes's universal principle of inertia implied that 'things which move in a circle always tend to recede from the centre of the circle that they describe'.[27] As he saw, this posed the question of why the planets do not fly off at a tangent and move away from the sun in a straight line. In anticipation of Newton, Descartes said that their tendency to fly off was counteracted by the fact that they were constantly falling towards the sun because of gravity.

According to Cartesian physics, gravity is due to circular motions of vortices (*tourbillons*). These were like whirlpools or whirlwinds rotating faster at the periphery than at the centre. Just as scraps of paper tend to move towards the centre of whirlpools and whirlwinds, so, according to Descartes, all bodies tend to move towards the centre of a vortex. One massive vortex carried the planets round the sun, and a subsidiary vortex carried the earth and the moon round the earth's axis, caused tides, and was responsible for the weight of bodies on earth. This theory also gave a reason why all the planets go round the sun in the same direction, and a reason why the moon goes round the earth's axis in the same direction as the earth.

As a young man (probably before 1619) Descartes had thought it impossible to explain the phenomenon of gravitation in terms of more fundamental properties of matter. He had regarded gravity as a 'real quality'. In retrospect, however, he saw this view as incompatible with the true principles of physics. It was not mechanistic: it involved action at a distance and, as he saw it, final causes: 'I used to think that gravity carried bodies towards the centre of the earth, as though it had some knowledge of this centre.'[28] Without something like the vortex theory the problem of explaining gravitation would have made the new mechanistic ideal of scientific explanation unworkable.[29]

It was therefore a very important event when Newton stated conclusive reasons for rejecting the vortex theory.[30] He pointed out that it could not explain why things gravitated towards the north and south poles; that it was incompatible with the observed differences in the frequency with which planets went round the sun, with the existence of comets and with Kepler's laws relating the paths and velocities of planets. In the *Principia* Newton set aside Descartes's ambition of reducing gravity to more fundamental properties of matter, and so managed to produce a wonderfully successful mathematical theory based on the idea that there was an 'attractive force' which was a universal property of matter. To many of Newton's disciples, Newton's success in this project made Descartes's obsession with mechanical reduction seem foolish and irrelevant. They saw no reason why gravity or attraction should not be regarded as a 'primary property of all bodies'.[31]

Newton's own position was more like that of the Cartesians than that of the Newtonians. This was not evident from the text of the first edition of the *Principia* (1686); but in subsequent writings Newton often drew attention to the fact that though he had said that attraction was a 'universal property' he had not said that it was 'essential and inherent to matter'. He claimed that his theory expressed the 'laws and properties of attraction', without explaining 'the cause by which attraction is performed'.[32] Newton was upset when certain disciples of his, like Bentley, ignored this feature of his position. He wrote to Bentley:

You sometimes speak of gravity as essential and inherent to matter. Pray do not ascribe that notion to me; for the Cause of Gravity is what I do not pretend to know.[33]

In a further letter he said:

That gravity should be innate, inherent, and essential to Matter, so that one Body may act upon another at a Distance thro a Vacuum, without the mediation of anything else, by and through which their action and force may be conveyed from one to another, is to me so great an absurdity, that I believe no man who has in Philosophical Matters a competent Faculty of Thinking, can ever fall into it.[34]

Since Descartes's vortex theory was inadequate, Newton had to seek other mechanical theories to take its place. These, like the vortex theory, had to be based on the idea that gravity might be explained in terms of the pressure of particles in some pervasive material medium.[35] Newton admitted that his suggestions were mere guesswork, however, and he was never satisfied with any of them. Unfortunately it was not until long after the first edition of *Principia* that he publicly disowned the idea that gravity is an irreducible property of matter.[36] By this time his attitude had been misinterpreted by his most influential disciples and the misinterpretation continues to this day.

The central principle of Cartesian physics is that the quantity of movement (later called momentum) in a closed system is constant.[37] Cartesian theory, like modern theory, defined momentum as the product of quantity of matter and rate of movement.[38] Owing to its identification of matter and space, however, its account of both these concepts was extremely complicated.

In modern theory, the rate of movement which is a factor of momentum is identified with speed in a specified direction, or velocity. In Cartesian theory, however, it is identified with a quantity which can be evaluated without reference to direction – that is, with something more like speed, or possibly energy.[39] At first sight, this appears to threaten to destroy Descartes's whole system of physical theory. It appears to leave open the possibility that all the particles in the universe might stampede in one direction; and this either involves the incoherent idea of the universe as a whole moving, or it means that the universe is losing momentum, and therefore that the laws of nature are being violated. In fact, however, there is no danger of Cartesian physics getting into this difficulty. The theory that all motions are 'in a way circular' rules out the possibility of a stampede, since it implies that any movement in one direction must be counteracted by an equal movement in the opposite direction.

This still left Cartesian physics with an intractable problem about the concept of rate of movement, if this was not to be identified with velocity. According to Cartesian theory, if I push a book across a table then I initiate a movement not only of the book but also of the entire ring of bodies which move with it; and the quantity of movement which I initiate will be a function of the mass of this entire ring. But there could be no non-arbitrary way of drawing a boundary round such a ring, since the effects of any given movement might reach out infinitely in space and time. Thus, in the context of Cartesian theory the concepts of mass and momentum became, for practical and experimental purposes, completely useless. The problem was aggravated by the fact that in Cartesian theory quantity of matter, or mass, was identified with volume or extension. In order to explain why some materials seem massier, volume for volume, than others, Descartes had implicitly to distinguish real from apparent volume. An individual piece or particle of matter was defined as 'whatever we consider as having a simple equal movement'[40] or 'whatever moves in one piece',[41] and a light material was thought of as containing particles in its interstices which did not share in its movements, and hence as having a smaller volume than it appeared to. This meant that the measurement of mass depended on the identification of movements, as well as the other way round; and this made the application of Cartesian theory even more problematic.

The identification of matter and space does not just complicate the Cartesian science of matter and motion; it makes it completely unworkable. Descartes had argued that every criterion for distinguishing matter and space which had ever been suggested was, for one reason or another, unsatisfactory. For instance he had argued that solidity and impenetrability could not be essential to matter, since when something is pulverized or liquefied it stops being solid and impenetrable without stopping being a piece of matter.[42] Unfortunately Descartes did not realize that it was necessary for him to provide some criterion for distinguishing matter from space. His idea that an individual particle of matter could be distinguished from its environment simply on the basis of having a movement which its environment does not share does not make sense: one has to single out the particle from its environment *before* one can detect its movements. Contrary to what Descartes assumed, one piece of space cannot move relative to another.

Descartes was extremely nonchalant about the relationship of his physical theories to facts established by observation (see above, p.43); and at the one point where he seriously tried to formulate useful mathematical laws, he failed spectacularly. In the *Principles*, he listed seven 'Rules of Impact', claiming, rather implausibly, that they followed from his three laws of nature.[43] Most of these rules are contradicted by obvious facts of everyday experience. Descartes may have been partly aware of these defects. He thought his theories applied to unresisted movements in a vacuum, but since he thought vacuum was

impossible, he could not expect his theories to be directly confirmed by experience. In addition, his denial of vacuum made
the basic quantities of his physics practically unmeasurable, so
he could not expect precise mathematical relationships between
them to be ascertainable in practice. The seven rules of impact,
he said, are 'extremely difficult to apply, because any given
body is always in contact with many others'.[44]

Newton succeeded in doing what Descartes had tried and
failed to do. He worked out precise and accurate mathematical
statements about the motions of particles, and these could be
applied directly to concrete situations which could be studied
in detail by observation and experiment. The very title of
Newton's main work, the *Philosophiae Naturalis Principia
Mathematica* was a reproach to Descartes's *Principia Philosophiae*. Newton's consequent contempt for Descartes verged
on hatred.[45] He even loathed Descartes's work in algebra and
geometry.[46] To some extent Newton's attitude was due to the
fact that it seemed to him that Cartesian physics left no room
for the activity of God in the physical world (see below, p.151).
But it was mainly due to Descartes's careless attitude to
observational accuracy and mathematical precision. Newton
thought that whereas he himself had derived his theories from
the facts of experience, Descartes systematically ignored them.
Newton's view of his relationship to Descartes is normally
accepted by historians of philosophy and science: but in fact it
is seriously inaccurate. It misrepresents both the extent and the
nature of their agreement, and of Newton's debts to Descartes.
Both of them were opponents of Aristotelianism, and this was
not essentially an opposition to those who ignored the facts of
experience. On the contrary, the trouble with the Aristotelian
tradition was that it relied too much on the facts of experience.
The Aristotelians had put the common-sense, everyday distinctions between motion and rest, between motion in a circle
and motion in a straight line, between violent and natural
motion, and between motion on earth and motion in the
heavens, at the basis of their physical theory, and they had
learnt from experience to think of motion, not as something

which was subject to conservation principles, but as something which naturally destroyed itself. This common sense had to be overthrown to make way for science. Descartes's lasting achievement as a physicist is that he constructed new, non-Aristotelian concepts of matter and motion, and declared that matter and motion were conserved quantities, to which all sorts of physical phenomena could be reduced. Newton's physical theory was to a large extent built on these foundations laid by Descartes.

Even in Newton's presentation, the new concepts of matter and motion could not be said to be derived from, or directly based on, observations or experiments. The idea of an inertial motion, continuing uniformly in a straight line for ever, which Newton took over from Descartes, lies quite beyond the bounds of experience and, indeed, of physical possibility.[47] Similarly, no experience, however bizarre, would disprove the principle of the conservation of momentum. If it appeared that momentum was being lost from a closed system, this would

---

Aristotle merely formulated the most commonplace experiences in the matter of motion as universal scientific propositions, whereas classical mechanics, with its principle of inertia and its proportionality of force and acceleration, makes assertions which not only are never confirmed by everyday experience, but whose direct experimental verification is fundamentally impossible.

Dijksterhuis[48]

---

not cast doubt on the conservation principle. It would simply raise the question whether the system was really closed, cast doubt on the definition of momentum and suggest that momentum was capable of taking some unsuspected form. So while Newtonian physical theory superseded much of Cartesian physical theory, it was in the Cartesian tradition.

The status of the conservation principles was and remains highly problematic. As one writer asked in the seventeenth century: 'Do our senses teach us how motion can pass from one body to another? Why there is transferred only a part of it, and why a body cannot communicate its motion in the same manner as a teacher communicates his knowledge, without losing any of that which he gives?'[49] Some writers have suggested that propositions like the conservation principles represent somewhat arbitrary choices to think in certain ways, and are not really descriptions of the world at all.[50] But this agnostic attitude was not shared by Descartes. He said that he would postulate them 'even if everything which affected our senses in the real world were contrary' to them.[51] The only direct argument he gave on this subject was that they followed from the fact that God is immutable, and that 'always acting in the same way, he always produces the same effect'.[52] This is clearly a very bad argument. If it was convincing, it would suggest that nothing at all ever changes. It does nothing to explain why motion should be subject to conservation principles while things like knowledge are not. However, Descartes seems to allude to other reasons for believing his laws: 'I tell you my reasons satisfy me on this question', he wrote, 'but I need not tell them to you yet.'[53] His attempt to state conclusive reasons for his laws preoccupied him until his death; and it carried him far away from physical theory, into investigations of God, knowledge and the mind.

[5]

Descartes's Early Concept of Ideas

The traditional, Aristotelian, approach to science had treated the universe as a closed system, in which irreducibly different types of beings each had their special place. Plants, animals, men, angels and God all had their position in a hierarchy which pervaded the universe. This approach had its counterpart in the elaborate patterns of social and economic relationships which existed in pre-capitalist societies. In the seventeenth century, at the economic level, these structures were being dissolved by the universal medium of money. And at the theoretical level, the new approach to science, pioneered by Descartes, had a similar effect. It dissolved the irreducible, specific, natures of things in the universal medium of the fundamental properties of matter.

The new approach to science had frightening implications, since it suggested that it was a mistake to think that men had a unique and privileged position in the universe. It suggested that the universe was a boundless and purely mechanical system, in which everything was reducible to matter and motion, and where nothing had any intrinsic superiority over anything else. It even suggested that human nature itself might be reducible to a few universal, quantitative, properties of matter. The idea that nature contains a rich variety of curious, irreducible and unique forms, and that it was made for man, came to seem like a superstitious projection of pre-scientific hopes and fears.

Biological theory was particularly vulnerable to the rise of this new approach to science. It had traditionally been assumed that the subject-matter of biology – human and animal bodies – could only be explained by using special concepts and principles quite different from those which applied to inanimate things. Descartes was convinced that this assumption was mistaken. In a section of *The World* called the *Treatise on Man*, he put forward the view that there was nothing about the human body which could not be reduced to the same physical basis as stars, rainbows, plants, sticks and stones. Even the most intricate and mysterious parts of the human body, the sense organs and the nerves, he argued, could be explained in a completely mechanistic way, and reduced to the law-governed movements of physical particles.[1]

Descartes believed that all the operations of the sense organs and the nerves were monitored and controlled by an organ at the centre of the nervous system – the tiny pineal gland at the base of the brain.[2] The overall purpose of his pioneering experimental and theoretical work on the nervous system was to show that all nervous activity begins or ends at this gland. He thought that the brain and the nerves contained tubes and cavities which were filled with a refined form of blood, which he referred to by the old-fashioned phrase 'animal spirits'. Minute movements of the pineal gland could affect the movements of the animal spirits which were constantly passing by or through the gland. Thus the gland could control the pressure of animal spirits in the part of the brain surrounding it. The nerves were hollow tubes filled with animal spirits and with an opening near the gland; so they transmitted the pressure variations brought about by the gland to every part of the body. The consequent pressure variations at the nerve-ends operated valves which triggered off muscular activity; and the result was that a physical action was performed.

Information from the sense organs, meanwhile, was supposed to be transmitted to the brain by means of cords which operated rather like old-fashioned bell-pulls, and which ran inside the same nerves. Suitable happenings in a sense organ tugged at these cords, which were connected at the other end with valves in the brain which regulated the flow of animal spirits there. When these alterations affected the pineal gland, the result was that the person perceived something.[3] Thus Descartes's neurophysiological theory tried to bring even human action and perception within the ambit of a universal science of matter and motion.

Descartes did not pursue his reductionist treatment of the human body to what might be considered its logical conclusion: the view that human beings are nothing but complicated machines. Instead, he claimed that the movements of the pineal gland, unlike the movements of other things, affected and were affected by the operations of a non-physical thing, the soul. He described the relation of the soul to the pineal gland and the animal spirits adjacent to it in just the way that one normally

---

When I consider the short duration of my life, swallowed up in the eternity of before and after, the little space which I fill, or indeed am able to see, engulfed in the infinite immensity of spaces of which I am ignorant, and which know me not, I am afraid ... The eternal silence of these infinite spaces frightens me.

Pascal[4]

---

describes the relation of an embodied person to his environment, speaking of it as perceiving and acting on the gland and the animal spirits. When a person performed an action, such as writing a letter, he was really acting on the animal spirits in his brain. He only acted on the pen and paper indirectly, by a sort of remote control. Similarly, when a person perceived something, such as a pen, he was really perceiving his animal spirits, rather than the pen itself. Thus, according to Descartes, the only things people perceived or acted on were things in their heads.

This view of the soul has been called the 'homunculus' theory, because it pictures the soul as a homunculus, or a little person, located inside the body, in some such organ as the brain or the heart.[5] It treats the observable behaviour of people's bodies as a sort of screen between the person and the outside world; and the face as a mask. To use an ancient, Platonistic image, it thinks of the soul as being in the body like a pilot in a ship. The homunculus concept of the soul is one of the most ancient and universal themes of philosophy. In fact the word 'body' derives from it, for originally it meant the 'binding' or wrapping of the soul. The attractions of the concept are threefold. First, it appeals to searchers after the consolations of religion because it suggests that you can escape from the harassments of earthly life by 'entering the chamber of the your mind'.[6] Secondly, it offers a vivid way of representing fact that a person's thoughts may not be revealed in his behaviour. For instance, it is used by Othello when he rails at Iago for behaving 'as if thou hadst shut up in thy brain some horrible conceit'.[7] Thirdly, it provides a unified account of correct perception, such as seeing real pink rats, and incorrect perception, such as seeing pink rats when in a state of *delirium tremens*. Descartes explained the relationship between such phenomena by saying that 'the same things which the soul perceives by means of the nerves (i.e. when something is really there to be seen) may also be represented by the fortuitous course of the animal spirits'.[8] The combination of mechanistic assumptions about biology with experimental evidence about the effects on perception of abnormal states of nerves and sense organs led most philosophers and scientists of the seventeenth and eighteenth centuries to think that the homunculus concept was absolutely unquestionable, and that people could not really act on or perceive anything except things in their brains.

Descartes stated emphatically and repeatedly that the soul has direct contact only with the pineal gland and the animal spirits surrounding it. He referred to the part of the brain where the soul was situated as the 'imagination' or the 'physical imagination'.[9] In his early writings, especially the *Rules*, *The World* and the *Dioptrics*,[10] he used a new technical term to refer to patterns of movements of the animal spirits in the imagination. This was the word 'idea'.[11] The word had been introduced into Western philosophy by Plato, who used it to refer to other-worldly archetypes, of which things in this world were imperfect imitations. Medieval theologians took it over and used it to denote archetypes of the mind of God. In Descartes's early works, however, it had very different connotations. Ideas were not other-worldly or divine, but entirely physical. 'I use the word "idea",' he wrote, 'to cover all the patterns which can be impressed on the spirits as they leave the gland.'[12] 'The imagination, together with its ideas, [is] an actual physical object, with extension and shape.'¹³ This use of the word 'idea' to refer to physical states of the brain probably derived from a usage which was then current, in which it meant roughly the same as 'pattern', 'plan' or 'copy'. 'Idea' was used in this sense, for example, when Buckingham said that Gloucester was the 'right idea' of his father,¹⁴ and it still retains this sense when it is used in the phrase 'musical idea'.¹⁵

According to the theory of ideas which Descartes put forward in his early work, to perform an action such as moving a leg is basically to act on the ideas in one's brain,¹⁶ and 'the *idea* of the movement of the limb is simply the way in which these spirits leave this gland'.¹⁷ Similarly, in perception 'it is the soul that sees, and not the eye, and it sees only through the medium of the brain':¹⁸ 'Only those [patterns] in the animal spirits at the surface of the gland should be considered as *ideas*, that is as the forms or images which the rational soul immediately contemplates.'¹⁹ Thus out of Descartes's homunculus concept of the soul there arose the theory that whenever a person perceives or acts on the world, he is using his ideas.

The influence of Descartes's concept of ideas has been enormous. Even today, discussions of thought, action and perception tend to be formulated with the help of the word 'idea' or derivatives of it like 'ideology', and however far removed they may be from Descartes's physiological theory, they are still indebted to it.

Apart from his own development of it in his later work, Descartes's early theory of ideas was developed in several different ways. In particular, one version of it became a central doctrine of the theoretical tradition which stems from Locke (1632–1704) and which is often called 'British Empiricism', although the positions typical of it were maintained more fervently by thinkers like Condillac in eighteenth-century France than they ever were in Britain. Philosophers in this tradition did not always follow the young Descartes in explicitly identifying ideas with brain states. Some of them were

materialistic about ideas; some were not; but most were indifferent or equivocal on the question, or at least only expressed
their answer in vague or metaphorical language. For instance
the psychologist Hartley (1705–57) wrote as follows: 'The
white medullary substance of the brain is also the immediate
Instrument by which Ideas are presented to the mind; or in
other words, whatever changes are made in this substance,
corresponding changes are made in our Ideas, and *vice-versa*.'[20]

Whether or not they thought that ideas were physical states
of the brain, the philosophers in this tradition agreed on an
important common doctrine, which can be called the empiricist
theory of mind (or of ideas). (It is also sometimes called
representationism, representative idealism, idea-ism, or idealism.) The empiricist theory of mind yields both an account of
action and an account of perception, but the 'British Empiricists'
were mainly interested in producing an account of perception.
They thought of a person's ideas as constituting a private
'world', and they thought of everything else as an 'external
world'. A person's perception of this 'external world' depended
on two separate abilities: his ability to recognize his ideas and
his ability to connect his ideas with things in the 'external
world'. A person had to identify his ideas first and then link
them with external objects.

Although the empiricist theory of mind was, and to some
extent still is, extremely influential,[21] it has long been realized
that it is completely bankrupt, both as a theory of action and
as a theory of perception. Suppose I think of Vienna. According
to the empiricist theory of ideas, the explanation of this is that
I have, or perceive, a certain idea – the idea of Vienna. But
how am I supposed to recognize my idea as an idea of Vienna?
The young Descartes might have said that people recognize
their ideas by being aware of their shape and size. Hume took
over this line of thought and suggested that ideas can be
identified by their position in or path through the brain. He
thought of people's ideas as being stored in a sort of library in
their heads waiting to be fetched by the animal spirits when
they were required:

The mind is endow'd with the power of exciting any idea it pleases, whenever it despatches the spirits into that part of the brain, in which the idea is plac'd.

Hume then went on to suggest that errors in reasoning occur when people mistake the identity of their ideas:

The animal spirits, falling into contiguous traces, present other related ideas, in lieu of that, which the mind at first desir'd to survey. This change we are not always sensible of, but continuing still in the same train of thought, make use of the related idea, which is presented to us, as if it were the same with what we demanded.[22]

These passages clearly reveal the poverty of the empiricist theory of ideas. In them Hume assumes that people can 'continue still in the same train of thought', even if they are having the wrong ideas, and that they can have a desire to 'survey' a particular idea even when it is absent. But this amounts to saying that people can have thoughts which cannot be explained in terms of their ideas; so ideas, as empiricists conceive of them, turn out to be unnecessary for thought.[23] In effect the empiricist theory tries to explain how people perceive and act on the 'external world' in terms of a supposed ability to perceive and act on an 'internal world'. So it leaves perception and action themselves completely unexplained.

It is not inconceivable that ideas as empiricists conceive of them should exist. For example, there could be human beings whose nervous systems were abnormal in such a way that they could feel things happening in their brains, just as normal people can feel things happening in their mouths, throats, limbs and so on. Such people might be able to recognize the occurrences in their brains which went with thinking of Vienna, just as normal people can recognize the occurrences in their mouths which go with thinking of sucking a lemon. But contrary to what the empiricist theory of ideas suggests, such abnormal abilities would not in themselves make one better able to think about or control the 'external world'. In general, the empiricist account of action and perception completely misrepresents the relationship between thinking about objects and thinking about ideas. Moreover, if the account were true, then thinking about anything except the private world of one's own ideas would be impossible. However hard one tried to think of an object with which to link an idea, one would never succeed in thinking of anything but an idea. The empiricist theory of ideas, in the words of Coleridge, 'places us in a dream world of phantoms and spectres, the inexplicable swarm and equivocal generation of our own brains'.[24]

Although the empiricist theory is, historically speaking, a development of Descartes's theory of ideas, it completely contradicts his original purpose. Descartes constructed the concept of ideas in order to explain the meaning of theoretical activity, and in particular to give an account of the relationship between the common-sense mentality which tries to understand the physical world in terms of categories based on sense experience, and the scientific outlook which tries to understand it in terms of the universal dimensions of matter (see below, p.89. The concept of ideas enabled him to say that thinking about the physical world always involves the formation of ideas in the physical imagination. The way to produce scientific knowledge was to replace common-sense ideas with scientific ones. The *Rules for the Direction of the Mind* was in effect a manual of techniques for bringing about the formation of such ideas:

The ideas must be formed as distinctly as possible in the imagination. The best thing to do is to get the very thing the idea is to represent and display it to the external senses . . . But if one wants to abstract (*deducat*) one from many . . . one should not present the things themselves to the senses, but rather certain symbols or diagrams of them.[25]

The *Rules* explained the use of diagrams to transmit information to the animal spirits in the imagination in such a way that the right sort of ideas would form themselves there.

Thus whereas Descartes conceived of ideas as more or less adequate tools or instruments which people use in order to think about and control the physical world, the empiricist theory treated ideas as constituting the only world people could directly perceive and act on. The world of ideas itself became an 'external world'. Ideas were placed beyond criticism as the only possible foundations of knowledge. Thus the concept of ideas came to fight on the side of theoretical reaction rather than theoretical change. Ideas became the end rather than the means of knowledge. The remarkable feature of Descartes's late philosophy is that on the whole it avoided the mistakes of the empiricist theory of ideas.

[6]

Doubt and the Soul

The character of Descartes's thinking changed considerably in the course of his life. The doctrines I have discussed up to this point all belong to his early life, when he was mainly concerned with working out the implications for physics of his reductionist ideal of scientific explanation. His remarks about subjects other than physics were rather careless, though they contained in a primitive form one very important notion – the notion of ideas. But in his later life, although he did not give up working on problems in physics, he became preoccupied with questions about human nature and knowledge. His main aim in his later work was to prove that human nature is such that human beings can, by observing the rules of method, attain scientific knowledge of the physical world. His investigation of the issues this raised forced him to transform many of his philosophical views.

The best place to draw a line between Descartes's early phase and his late phase is about 1630, when he was in his middle thirties, had worked out most of his physics, and had emigrated to Holland in the hope of devoting the rest of his life to research.[1] Descartes often concealed the changes which his thought underwent not only from other people, but also from himself; and there was no sharp break between his early philosophy and his late philosophy. His thought developed like a forest where dying trees stand unnoticed in the midst of vigorous young ones which have grown from their seeds.

The seed of what was new in Descartes's late philosophy is what has come to be known as the method of doubt, which Descartes worked out in 1629 or 1630, and which he explained most fully in the *Meditations*, a series of six brief Latin essays which he published in 1641. These essays purport to be the spontaneous diary of six days of intense thinking, but their appearance of simplicity is deceptive. They were in fact drafted and redrafted countless times over a period of eleven years.[2]

The method of doubt is a technique for identifying the essences of things. The word 'essence' here simply means what corresponds to a thing's definition. In this sense, if a person is defined as a rational animal, it follows that only animality and rationality belong to a person's essence, and therefore that anything which is both rational and an animal is a person. The method of doubt is based on the principle that if you can doubt whether a certain thing has a given property, then that property cannot be essential to the thing, so that if you wanted to find out whether rationality really was part of the essence of a person you could try to doubt the existence of rationality without doubting the existence of persons. In other words, you could try to conceive of a person who lacked rationality. If you could do so, this would prove that rationality was not essential to being a person. Thus doubt is an acid for etching away what does not belong to a thing's essence. The 'conceivability tests' which modern analytical philosophers use to investigate the relationships of concepts are a modern equivalent of Descartes's method of doubt.[3]

The method of doubt (like the use of conceivability tests) is fraught with difficulties, because the notion of what can be doubted (or conceived) is extremely complex. Saying that one doubts something, or even sincerely believing that one does so, does not prove that it can be doubted. If someone said 'Human beings are undoubtedly descended from apes', he would not mean that nobody had actually said or thought that he doubted it. This has led some people to think that the method of doubt cannot prove anything at all; or that at best it can only reveal what one thinks the essences of things are, and not what they really are.[4] As the young theologian Arnauld (1612–94) pointed out in his contribution to the set of *Objections* and *Replies* which were published along with the *Meditations*, it is plausible to say that one might manage to think of a right-angle triangle while doubting whether Pythagoras's theorem applies to it.

(That is, one might think of a right-angle triangle while doubting whether the square on its hypotenuse was equal to the squares on its other two sides.) But, as Arnauld observed, this would not prove that there could conceivably be a right-angle triangle to which Pythagoras's theorem does not apply.[5] This objection, however, is only an objection to using the method of doubt carelessly. Arnauld's point proves that the applicability of Pythagoras's theorem to a right-angle triangle cannot really be doubted; it does not prove that the method of doubt is useless.[6] It will be met provided it is remembered that for the purposes of the method of doubt dubiousness has to be proved, rather than dogmatically asserted.

A further criticism of techniques like the method of doubt was developed by Wittgenstein, who objected to the whole project of seeking definitions for ordinary concepts: 'We are unable clearly to circumscribe the concepts we use; not because we don't know their real definition, but because there is no real "definition" to them. To suppose that there must be would be like supposing that whenever children play with a ball they play games according to strict rules.'[7] This objection is misconceived. It may be true that there is a certain amount of disorder in the use of everyday words. But since words would be useless for communicating information if speaker and audience did not recognize them as being used in accordance with rules which both of them know, there is every reason for wanting to keep this disorder down to a minimum. One way of doing this is to use conceivability tests or the method of doubt.

Another thing to remember about the method of doubt is that it cannot create definitions out of nothing. One could not try to work out a definition of human beings, for instance, unless one had a rough idea of what human beings are before one began. One would have to begin with a preliminary definition, for otherwise it would not be clear what one was setting out to define. The only legitimate use for the method of doubt is to refine preliminary definitions or make them more precise.

Descartes stated that his aim in the *Meditations* was to apply the method of his physics to questions concerning God and the soul. He had turned his attention to such questions in response to requests from people 'who knew that I had developed a certain method for solving all sorts of scientific problems ... which ... I had applied rather successfully to other difficult problems'.[8] Elsewhere, he said that he had 'only used analysis in the *Meditations*'.[9]

Descartes's analytical method consisted in redescribing more 'relative' phenomena in terms of less 'relative' ones (see above, p.37). This involved describing composite natures in terms of simple ones, or reducing the composite to the simple. The results of analysis were to be expressed in formulae which equated the composite nature with a specific combination of simple natures. In the *Meditations*, the counterpart of the

---

After I had spent several years in thus studying the book of the world and trying to get experience, I decided one day to study within myself as well.

Descartes[10]

---

method of analysis is the method of doubt. Descartes illustrated this in the First Meditation, where he used the method of doubt, in a sketchy way, to discover the essence of physical things. He noticed that he could doubt the existence of particular composite natures in the physical world, such as his hands, without doubting the existence of objects which were 'more simple and more general'. These 'real and true' objects were the physical simple natures.[11] Thus the method of doubt was used by Descartes for identifying dependencies of composite natures on simple ones: it was a less technical form of his analytical method in physics.[12]

In the *Meditations* Descartes was not primarily concerned with discussing the essence of material things. His main object was to investigate the essence of human nature: to define the real human person, or the human soul. He explained his starting-point in the *Discourse on Method*, saying that he adopted the method of doubt in the hope of expelling from his mind all the rubbish that had accumulated there since he was a child:

> I thought I ought to . . . reject as absolutely false everything which I could imagine the slightest reason for doubting, in order to see if there was anything left . . . which was entirely indubitable.[13]

He wondered whether he might be a victim of perceptual illusions, or whether perhaps his whole life was a dream. But as he drifted in the ocean of uncertainty which these thoughts carried him into, he noticed what seemed like a solid rock of truth:

> I realised that, even as I tried in this way to suppose that every-thing was false, it was absolutely necessary that I, who was doing the thinking [*qui le pensais*] was something. And noticing that this truth, 'I think therefore I am', was so firm and assured that the most extravagant scepticism could not shake it, I concluded that I might accept it, without hesitation, as the first principle of the philosophy I sought.[14]

Descartes was not claiming that the truth of every other proposition really was doubtful: in fact much of his later philosophy was devoted to disproving such scepticism. His purpose in using the method of doubt was to draw attention to the fact that even if one had good reasons for a general sceptical doubt, one would never have any reason for doubting that one was thinking. However much one dreams up extrava-gant hypotheses to cast doubt on the truth of one's thoughts about the rest of the world, one never has any reason for doubting that one is having thoughts. Indeed, the attempt to deny that one is thinking is nonsensical: it is doomed by being undertaken, since denying that one is thinking, like denying anything else, actually involves thinking. Thus one's knowledge that one thinks differs from one's knowledge of other things. Thinking is peculiarly and uniquely indubitable: 'I am not wholly certain of any of my activities except one: thinking.'[15]

Descartes sometimes used the words '*cogito ergo sum*' ('I think therefore I am') to express this peculiar certainty.[16] Although they do not occur in the *Meditations*, these words have acquired an extraordinary fame; and it has even been assumed that they somehow epitomize the whole of Descartes's philosophy. This gives the unfortunate impression that Descartes's main concern was to prove that he existed – which would have been an extremely bizarre thing to have wanted to do.[17] In fact his purpose was to explain what it meant to say that he existed – to define himself, or in other words to discover his essence or his soul.

In order to understand the conclusion Descartes was arguing for, it is necessary to be aware of the relationship between the concept of the soul and the concept of mind. Ever since their emergence in Western thought in the sixth and fifth centuries B.C.[18] these two concepts have been closely related. Both of them have normally been applied to 'spiritual' or 'higher' qualities, as opposed to 'animal' or 'base' ones; to intellectual as opposed to sensory experience; to reason as opposed to emotion; to the immortal as opposed to the mortal attributes; to the truly and eternally valuable, as opposed to the mundane details of everyday life. But up to the seventeenth century at least, the meanings of the words 'soul' and 'mind' were quite distinct. 'Mind' (*mens, ingenium, esprit, entendement*) had intellectual connotations; in fact many writers, including Descartes on some occasions, used 'intellect' as a synonym for 'mind'. 'Mind', which is etymologically related to 'meaning', meant something quite like 'thought' or 'opinion'; and it still has this sense today in phrases like 'speaking your mind'.[19] 'Soul' (*anima, âme*), on the other hand, was part of the vocabulary of religion, and had very close links with the notion of life. The soul was what did good or evil deeds, what might survive bodily death, and what could be either damned or saved. The soul, in short, was the essence of the person. Since the eighteenth century the meanings of 'soul' and 'mind' have grown much closer to each other. For instance, Bishop Berkeley found it quite natural to speak of the being which 'I call mind, spirit, soul, or myself'.[20] The old concept of the soul is now better expressed by the words 'person', 'ego' and 'self'.[21]

According to the definition of the human soul which Descartes put forward in his late philosophy, the soul just *is* the mind. Descartes realized that this definition – which I will call the idealist definition of the soul – would strike his readers as very strange; in fact he claimed that, as far as he knew, no one had ever put it forward before,[22] but he thought he had produced a conclusive argument for it. The premiss of the argument was that one could deny the existence of everything except one's mind, without thereby denying the existence of one's soul; in other words that it is conceivable that the individual soul should exist even if nothing but thinking or the mind existed. If this premiss is true then, assuming that the method of doubt is legitimate, Descartes would obviously be justified in concluding that the soul is nothing more than thinking or the mind. It would follow, to put it in his own words, that human beings are 'something whose whole essence consists entirely in thinking'.[23] 'Strictly speaking, then, I am nothing but a thing that thinks – that is, a mind, soul, intellect or reason.'[24]

Locke thought that Descartes had completely failed to justify his idealist definition of the soul. His comment was: 'It is but defining the soul to be "a substance which thinks" and the business is done.'[25] There is some justice in this criticism, for the premiss and the assumption of Descartes's argument are highly questionable. But the argument has to be approached by a rather roundabout route. It can only be understood when Descartes's identification of the mind with the soul has been related to his highly original account of the nature of mind.

Descartes's Late Concept of Ideas

One of the fields in which Descartes applied his account of the soul was the theory of knowledge. He used it in order to discuss the belief that there are two kinds of knowledge, one belonging to the mind or intellect, the other to the senses and perhaps also the imagination. This dualism of sensory and intellectual knowledge can be called Platonistic dualism, although Plato himself withheld the title of 'knowledge' from sensory knowledge.[1] On the Platonistic view, sensory knowledge is concerned with the 'sensible world', which contains concrete particulars like my house or a sunny day or a triangle drawn on a piece of paper. According to many theories, sensory knowledge depends exclusively on bodily organs and is shared by human beings with animals. Intellectual knowledge, on the other hand, is concerned with the 'intelligible world' which contains abstract universals such as manhood, the good and triangularity.

In a modified form, the Platonistic dualism was retained not only by Aristotle but also by scholastic Aristotelians. Thus, St Thomas Aquinas wrote that, 'The senses are bodily powers and know singulars tied down to matter, whereas mind is free from matter and knows universals which are abstract from matter and contain limitless instances.'[2] Although the scholastics, unlike Plato, attached great importance to sensory experience, and claimed that it was impossible to obtain intellectual knowledge without first acquiring sensory knowledge, they did not question the Platonistic dualism and sensory and intellectual knowledge.

In a fragment dating from his twenty-third year, Descartes himself adopted a form of Platonistic dualism. He stressed the difference between knowledge of sensible things, like wind, light, movement and heat, and knowledge of what he called the 'Olympica', 'spiritual things' or 'the heights' – that is, of subjects like mind, life, knowledge, love and creation. Like the scholastics, he said that the path to intellectual knowledge lay through sensory knowledge:

Just as the imagination uses shapes for conceiving bodies, so the intellect uses certain sensible bodies to represent spiritual things . . . One is more likely to find weighty thoughts in the writings of poets than of philosophers. This is because poetry is subject to enthusiasm and the force of imagination . . . Sensible things are apt for conceiving the *Olympica* – wind represents spirit; movement in time, life; light, knowledge; heat, love; instantaneous activity, creation . . . In our opinion, the philosopher who assimilates problems [*res quaesitas*] to things known by the senses is the one who gets closest to the truth.[3]

After he had written this passage Descartes developed his early theory of ideas, which identified ideas with physical patterns in the brain, and said they were essential for knowledge of the natural world (see above, pp.64-65). This theory of ideas led him to discard his earlier version of the distinction between 'sensible' and 'spiritual' matters and, in the first instance, to replace it with a distinction between knowledge of the physical and of the mental systems of natures. In this brief transitional phase, he seems to have thought that the main difference between the two types of knowledge was that knowledge of physical things involved ideas, whereas knowledge of mental things did not. Things which were 'purely mental' (*pure intellectuales*) were 'known by a certain natural (*ingenitum*) light, and without the help of any physical images (*imaginis*)'.[4] Mathematics, according to Descartes, was not mental or intellectual in this sense it was a form of physical knowledge. This is why he thought it important to visualize real physical counterparts to mathematical operations (see above, pp.28-29). But in the *Rules* he found it extremely difficult to give a clear account of his reasons.

Even if it is possible to believe that, e.g., supposing every extended thing in the universe were annihilated, there would still be such a thing as extension itself, this conception would not make use of any physical idea (*idea corporea*), but only of the intellect making faulty judgements.[5]

This is one of the most awkward sentences Descartes ever wrote; and the complicated formulation betrays uneasiness. His reference to the conceivability of annihilating everything in the universe without annihilating extension foreshadows the method of doubt, which he had not yet formulated explicitly. Shortly after this Descartes gave up work on the manuscript of the *Rules*, and also abandoned the Platonistic dichotomy between sensory and intellectual knowledge. He then entered the period of his philosophical maturity.

Descartes completed work on the *Meditations* about twelve years after abandoning the *Rules*. In the Second Meditation he discussed an example which, from the Platonistic point of view, would be classified as knowledge by 'bodily powers' as opposed to 'mental knowledge'. He enumerated various 'sensible properties' of a particular piece of beeswax – its colour, shape and size, its coldness and hardness, its sweet taste of honey and its scent of flowers. Then he pointed out that when the wax was moved near the fire, its colour, shape and size altered, it lost its sweetness and its fragrance disappeared. In spite of these changes, however, it was obviously the same piece of wax.

Descartes thought that anyone who accepted the Platonistic dichotomy between the sensible world and the intelligible world would be unable to explain this continuity through change.[6] A Platonistic explanation, he believed, would involve thinking of sensible properties as resembling sets of clothes, which an underlying body with a constant set of intelligible properties can change from time to time.[7] It is not certain whom Descartes thought he was arguing against; but Aquinas had at least toyed with the notion that 'accidental properties' could be thought of as capable of being removed from a thing to reveal the 'naked substance' underneath. 'The naked substance,' he had said, 'can be grasped only by the mind: the senses cannot reach it.'[8] In criticizing this Platonistic notion of an intelligible body clothed with sensible properties, Descartes assumed that the 'intelligible properties' of the 'naked substance' could be identified with the properties of occupying space and of being malleable and flexible. He then argued that, if it was interpreted in this way, one aspect of the Platonistic theory was correct; that properties such as extension, malleability and flexibility are known by the mind rather than by the body's physical powers. Descartes's argument was that our conceptions of such properties cannot be identical with any states of our body such as physical patterns in the brain (the 'physical ideas' of his early theory). To say that something is malleable and flexible is not to say anything specific about it, such as that it could be round, square or oblong; it is to say something very general about it, namely that it could assume any of an infinite number of shapes. And this generality, according to Descartes, could not possibly be a function of mere patterns in the animal spirits in the imagination: 'My imagination is incapable of encompassing this infinity, so my conception of the wax cannot have been produced by the faculty of imagination.' Having satisfied himself by this brief, and not entirely convincing, argument that the Platonistic theory is right in saying that the so-called 'intelligible properties' are known by the mind, Descartes went on to argue that it is wrong in trying to treat the so-called 'sensible properties' differently. Its account of the 'intelligible properties', he suggested, applied to 'sensible properties' too. After all, it would be strange if one and the same thing, namely the piece of wax, had two fundamentally different types of properties, known in completely different ways: 'What is this wax that can only be conceived by the mind? Surely it is the same thing that I see, touch, and imagine, and the same wax as I perceived at the outset?' Descartes's conclusion was that there was a need for a new theory of knowledge, which would avoid the problems which the Platonistic theory created, by denying that there are two completely different types of properties, known by distinct faculties. Knowledge of all sorts of properties should be ascribed to one and the same faculty: the mind, or the faculty of thinking. 'The point to notice is that the perception of it [i.e. of the piece of wax] is not a seeing, or a touching, or an imagining; nor has it ever been so, even though that is how it used to seem: it is nothing but a mental awareness.'[9] There was no such thing as knowledge which belonged to the senses rather than to the mind.

In some ways Descartes never completely freed himself from his old habits of thought. He continued to use the Platonistic dualism of sensory and intellectual knowledge in his late philosophy, though he came to give priority to intellectual knowledge rather than sensory knowledge; and he continued to think that the distinctive thing about 'purely mental' knowledge was that it did not depend on the special brain states he had once referred to as ideas. But in his later works, his use of the distinction between mental and physical knowledge was not very careful or consistent. On the one hand, he continued to think that mathematical or geometrical knowledge ought to be based on such brain states, though he no longer believed that it absolutely required them[10]; and on the other, he sometimes suggested that the fundamental variables of his physics could be distinguished from properties like colours and smells because they were known by the intellect or mind rather than by the senses.[11]

But these complications should not be allowed to conceal the fact that Descartes's late philosophy contained a magnificent achievement in the theory of knowledge. This achievement found expression in two alterations which he was forced to make to his early theory of ideas.

In the first place, he had to give up treating ideas as physical. His early theory of ideas had said that ideas were physical patterns in the brain which were perceived by the soul in the pineal gland. This implied that in order to think of, say, the scent of the wax, one had to get the right sort of physical ideas to form themselves in one's brain. But the exploration of the possibility of doubting everything showed that this was not so. Even if one had reasons for doubting the existence of the wax, or for that matter of one's body together with one's brain and physical ideas, one would have no reason to doubt that one was thinking of the scent of wax.[12] It was conceivable that one should think of something, even if one did not have a physical idea of it. In order to explain this possibility, Descartes altered his theory of ideas, by saying that ideas were *not* physical. At the risk of making him sound childish, one might say that he moved ideas out of the brain and into the soul.

The main works in which Descartes had stated his early theory of ideas (the *Rules* and *The World*) remained unfinished and were not published in his lifetime, so he was able to pretend that he had never held his early theory.[13] He now wrote that 'anyone who gave the matter the slightest consideration' would realize that:

the knowledge which one might possibly think of as most subject to our imagination, because it is concerned only with magnitudes and figures and movement, is not really based on its images at all, but only on the mind's . . . notions.

He also made the following announcement:

I do not use the word 'idea' for images in the imagination [*fantaisie*]; on the contrary I do not call these by this name at all if they are in the physical imagination [*fantaisie corporelle*]. In general, I apply the word 'idea' to whatever is in our mind when we conceive something, no matter how we conceive it.[14]

This new concept of ideas enabled him to avoid the inadequacies of the empiricist account of the mind.

The empiricist account of the mind treats ideas as *objects* of thought or perception. It suggests that identifying one's ideas and identifying the things they represent are exercises of different abilities, and that a person might conceivably have the ability to identify his ideas even if he did not see how to connect them with things in the 'external world' (see above, p.66-68). Descartes's late theory of ideas did not have this implication. It only implied that it must be possible to have an idea of a particular thing – such as the scent of wax – even if that thing does not exist. Thus Descartes was able to devote most of the *Meditations* to arguing that it is inconceivable that a person

should be able to identify his ideas without being able to connect any of them with things in the 'external world'. In his
late philosophy, he avoided treating ideas as objects of thinking,
which somehow intervened between the person and the
external world, preventing him from having direct knowledge
of it. To think was to have ideas; but thinking was not necessarily *about* ideas; the terms 'thought' and 'idea' became
practically interchangeable.[15]

The second way in which Descartes had to change his theory
of ideas was by generalizing it. According to his late theory,
ideas were involved in all thinking, whether about mathematical subjects, physical particulars, general characteristics of
the physical world, angels, imaginary beings or even God.
Ideas were what we have in mind when we conceive something,
no matter how we conceive it; that is, whether by the intellect or
the senses. Thus Descartes formulated for the first time the
ordinary modern notion of ideas, or concepts. The word
'concept' had been part of the terminology of the theory of
knowledge long before Descartes formulated his late theory of

---

*The modern concept of nature, as its shape becomes increasingly articulate
from the Renaissance on and as it seeks philosophical foundation and
justification in the great systems of the seventeenth century – in Descartes,
Spinoza, and Leibniz – is characterised above all by the new relationship
which develops between sensibility and intellect, between experience and
thought, between the sensible world and the intelligible world.*

Ernest Cassirer[16]

---

ideas, but it had been used in a more restricted way. Originally,
it expressed a comparison between the creation of knowledge
and sexual reproduction. In the Middle Ages, it had become a
technical term for that which is present in the intellect (or
rather 'possible intellect') when an intelligible property (or
rather 'intelligible species') was perceived. It would hardly
have made sense, on this theory, to talk of alternative concepts
of, say, colour, motion or heat, or to contrast scientific concepts with unscientific ones. This modern notion of concepts

was invented by Descartes who quite often used 'concept' and 'idea' as synonyms.[17]

Descartes's generalization of the notion of ideas caused considerable consternation to some of his contemporaries, particularly Hobbes, who had a concept of ideas similar to that of Descartes's early theory, and could not see how there could be ideas of things other than physical particulars.[18] Descartes was very impatient with Hobbes for misunderstanding him; but Hobbes's difficulty is not surprising. The new theory of ideas was based on the rejection of something which had always had a central place in theories of knowledge in the West. For centuries people had been regarded as having an intellect or mind for perceiving an intelligible world and senses for perceiving a sensible world. Descartes's innovation was to say that in fact people have one faculty for perceiving one world; and this theory was as original as a theory can be.

[8]

Ideas and Science

The Platonistic theory of knowledge was frequently used to interpret physical laws of nature, such as those put forward by Galileo, Descartes and Newton. According to the Platonistic interpretation, the fact that such laws expressed perfect mathematical regularities indicated that they referred to a suprasensible, perhaps divine, world of artifice and purpose, rather than to the chaotic flux of the sensible world. This interpretation was adopted by Galileo, who thought of laws of nature as resembling positive laws of the state and that physical particles were like law-abiding subjects. It was as though nature was an autocratic ruler whose edicts stated how particles must behave in various situations. The job of the scientist was to observe the behaviour of particles in the hope of inferring what nature's edicts were. Galileo admitted that since 'nature did not make human brains first, and then construct things according to their capacity of understanding' it might be very difficult to discover her 'reasons and methods of operating'; but he was convinced that she allowed men to 'ferret out a few of her secrets'.[1] 'Human wisdom understands some propositions as perfectly,' he said, 'and is as absolutely certain thereof, as Nature herself.'[2]

Many early physical scientists exploited this conception of laws of nature in order to argue that the regularities described by the new science could not be explained without reference to God. For instance the biologist John Ray (1627–1705) stated that 'They being but stupid and senseless matter, cannot of themselves continue any regular and constant motion, without the guidance and regulation of some intelligent Being.'[3] Similarly, Ralph Cudworth (1617–88) drew attention to 'the *Universality* and *Constancy* of this *Regularity*, and its long Continuance through so many ages, that there are no Records

85

Descartes

at all of the contrary any where to be found'. The view that this regularity could be explained without reference to God was 'the most *Prodigious Nonsense Imaginable*, and can be accounted no other, than *Atheistick Fanaticism*'.[4] Descartes and his followers – the '*Mechanick or Atomick Theists*', as Cudworth called them – were an even greater danger to religion than the '*Atomick Atheists*'.[5] Although they believed in the existence of God, they thought that, quite independently of divine planning, physical particles had 'taken up their Places, and ... Ranged themselves, so *Orderly*, *Methodically*, and *Discreetly*; as that they could not possibly have done it better, had they been directed by the most *Perfect Wisdom*'.[6] In this way, according to Cudworth, Descartes had sabotaged the best proofs of religion. By doing away with the Platonistic theory of knowledge, Descartes had cast doubt on the view that the laws which regulate nature must originate in an immaterial and suprasensible world, and that they are laid down and enforced by a divine legislator with a liking for geometry and mathematics.

Descartes's late concept of ideas enabled him to deny that mathematical knowledge is knowledge of a suprasensible world of intelligible objects, such as numbers and what the scholastics had called 'universals':

For number, considered in the abstract, or in general, is only a mode of thought; and the same applies to all other 'universals' ... Universals arise solely from the fact that we avail ourselves of one and the same idea in order to think of all the individual things which have some resemblance.[7]

According to Descartes, mathematical ideas, such as the ideas of a right-angle triangle or of a straight line or of growth according to a mathematical law, were like any other ideas in that their function was to represent properties of individual things. He was willing to admit that many mathematical ideas were what modern writers would call idealizations, because, for instance, no real line is absolutely and perfectly straight; but he did not conclude that mathematical properties had to be

86

placed in a special Platonistic realm of 'universals'. They were just as much properties of individual things as redness, heaviness and warmth.

Descartes realized that his ideal for physical science could only be achieved by criticizing the categories of common-sense sensory knowledge, such as the qualitative distinctions between colours, or between light and heat, and by replacing them with quantitative conceptions defined in terms of the universal properties of matter. Thus before expounding his

---

Even if he [Descartes] was mistaken about the laws of nature, at least he was the first to realise that there must be some.

d'Alembert[8]

---

theory that light of any colour is nothing but the oscillation of tiny particles, he stated that the common-sense distinctions between colours ought to be ignored because they only reflected esoteric facts about the human body.[9] He also argued that the physical basis of light was the same as that of heat, although the fact that heat and light are perceived by different senses suggests to unreflective common sense that they are fundamentally different. The main objection to the Platonistic dualism was that it suggested that general theoretical considerations applied to the intelligible world rather than the sensible world,[10] and that it thereby shielded the conceptions involved in ordinary sensory knowledge from scientific criticism.

The main difference between scientific and unscientific ideas, according to Descartes, was that scientific ideas were both clear, as opposed to obscure, and distinct, as opposed to confused, whereas unscientific ideas were not. In spite of their importance in his theory of science, Descartes used the concepts of clarity and distinctness and their opposites carelessly. Sometimes he applied them to ideas, sometimes to perceptions or judgements; sometimes, but not always, he suggested that one and the same idea can vary in clarity and distinctness; and sometimes, but not always, he suggested that the clarity and distinctness of an idea depends simply on what it is an idea of.

Descartes explained his notion of clarity by saying, 'I apply the word "clear" to what is present and apparent to an attentive mind . . . When a severe pain is felt, for instance, the perception of the pain may be very clear.'[11] Distinct perception presupposed clear perception, but it also required something more: 'The distinct is that which is so precise and different from all other objects that it contains within it nothing but what is clear.'[12] The meaning of 'distinct' is thus very close to that of 'separate' and 'independent'; and what makes an idea or perception confused is that it combines elements which ought to be kept separate. According to Descartes, perceptions based on the senses, whether of states of the body, like pains, or of 'sensible' properties, like warmth or redness, were never distinct, even though they might be clear (see below, pp.91-94).

This suggests that Descartes's concept of distinctness is an expression of the system-of-natures theory of science put forward in the *Rules*, according to which 'there is nothing to science (*humanam scientiam*) except seeing distinctly (*distincte*) how these simple natures run together to compose other things'[13] (see above, p.34). To perceive something distinctly, or to have a distinct idea of it, was to think of it in terms of the simple natures of which it is composed.[14] Descartes's examples of distinct ideas correspond either to what is simple – to the mind or soul, to physical substance,[15] to God[16] and to movement, size, duration and number[17] – or to things which are defined in terms of these. Although ordinary ideas of, say, heat and cold and colours were confused, they could be replaced with distinct ideas defined in terms of the simple natures.[18]

In his early work, Descartes explained his analytic method as a technique for sorting out absolutes from relatives, and of reducing composite natures to simple ones (see above, pp.36-38); in his late work he explained it as the technique of replacing confused ideas with ideas which were both clear and distinct.[19] He then summarized his method in what is known as the principle of clarity and distinctness, which, in the words of the

Discourse, is the 'general rule that the things we conceive very clearly and distinctly are all true'.[20] Many interpreters have thought that this principle amounted to the claim that mere subjective certainty, or mere personal faith, were enough to justify a claim to knowledge. As a result, they have depicted Descartes as a sort of Canute, suffering from delusions about the power of thought over reality. For example, Bertrand Russell dismissed the principle by saying: 'Empiricism has made such a view impossible; we do not think that even the utmost clarity of our thoughts would enable us to demonstrate the existence of Cape Horn.'[21] This criticism is misguided. Descartes never believed that anything like the existence of Cape Horn could be proved on the basis of the principle of clarity and distinctness. In general, the most that was proved by a person's having a clear and distinct idea of something was that it was *possible* for that thing to exist.[22]

In the *Meditations,* Descartes distinguished two types of truth and falsehood, formal and material. Formal truth and falsehood belonged to judgements, and material truth and falsehood to the ideas of which they were composed. Ideas were materially false when they 'represent what is nothing as though it were something'.[23] The ordinary concept of heat, according to Descartes, was of this kind. If I am conscious of the heat of the fire, then I am tempted to judge that there is something in the fire which is accurately represented by my idea of heat. But this temptation is to be resisted.

The ideas which I have of cold and heat are so far from clear and distinct that I cannot tell from them whether cold is merely the absence of heat, or heat the absence of cold, or whether each is a real quality, or whether neither is. And since (to the extent that ideas are analogous to images) all ideas purport to represent things, if cold is in fact nothing but the absence of heat, the idea which represents it to me as real and positive, deserves to be called false.[24]

So although the judgement that the fire contains heat is not formally false, since the fire really is hot rather than cold, it is still inaccurate because it involves a confused, unscientific, materially false idea of heat.

Descartes's concept of clear and distinct ideas enabled him to treat common-sense descriptions and scientific ones as belonging to different stretches of a single continuum, rather than as being separated by an absolute dichotomy and as referring to different worlds. Although science had to break with common sense, scientific investigation had to start from ordinary, confused experience of the natural world; it did not require acquaintance with another world, a suprasensible world of mathematical truths. The possibility of distinguishing science from common sense was due to the fact that a person's experience of something 'may be imperfect and confused ... or clear and distinct ... according as ... attention is directed more or less closely to the things of which it is composed'.[25] The scientist's task was to take ordinary experience and 'render it more distinct and explicit'.[26] But Descartes was forced to admit that 'it can be very difficult to see which things we conceive distinctly'.[27] The greatest difficulty was presented by human action and perception.

[9]

Mind and Body

Descartes thought that the majority of common-sense descriptions of the way people act on the world and perceive it were very obscure and confused. They were used for ascribing a combination of mental and physical states to people; so they were a sort of hybrid. For instance, being hungry is partly a matter of having the thought that you want something to eat, and partly a matter of having an empty stomach; looking at something involves both thinking about it and having it before your eyes so that it affects them in certain ways; and going for a walk consists partly in thinking of going for a walk and partly in your legs moving. Descartes realized that descriptions couched in this hybrid language played an important part in everyday life; and he also believed that it was inevitable that children should think in such terms[1]; but he thought that such descriptions ought to be excluded from scientific discourse, where the mental and physical aspects of human beings had to be carefully separated.[2]

One of Descartes's reasons for separating the mental and physical aspects of human beings was that he wanted to define an area in which everything could be completely explained by a reductionist, mechanistic physical science.[3] To the extent that ordinary descriptions of human beings – in terms of being hungry, looking at things, going for walks and so on – referred to physical states rather than mental ones, they were simply confused, unscientific descriptions of states which would be described best by a reductionist physics. There was nothing mysterious or spiritual about these physical states: they could occur in beings which could not think, like animals, machines and dead human bodies. It might be very difficult to give an accurate physical account of them. In fact, from the point of view of physics it might be a mistake to group them together.

The only feature they shared was that when they occur in the body of a human being they normally attract his attention to the presence of conditions which are either favourable or unfavourable to life and health,[4] and this obviously did not mean that they deserved to be put in a special category for the purposes of physical science.

Descartes's other reason for carefully separating the mental and physical aspects of human beings was that he was advocating unified explanation of mental states, to complement his unified explanation of physical states. His account of the mind was as reductionist as his account of the physical world. He opposed the view that human beings have several irreducibly disparate mental faculties, such as sense, intellect, will, memory and imagination – a view which can be labelled pluralism. In opposition to pluralism, he tried to reduce all these apparently disparate faculties to a single basis. He thought that all mental operations could be reduced to thinking, just as other things could be reduced to the fundamental properties of material substance.

Descartes gave his explanation of what thinking is in the Third Meditation. To have a thought was either to have a desire or aversion, or to make an assertion or denial; and desires and aversions, and assertions and denials, were combinations of ideas from each of the two 'faculties' of the mind, the intellect and the will.[5] It might be thought that in distinguishing between these two faculties Descartes was putting forward a pluralistic theory of the mind, rather than a reductionist theory. But in fact he did not regard the intellect and the will as independent of each other. On the contrary, he thought that they could only operate in collaboration. His explanation of mental phenomena is therefore similar to his reductionist explanation of physical phenomena: all mental phenomena could be reduced to intellect and will, just as all physical phenomena could be reduced to matter and motion. The 'faculties' of intellect and will were stores of ideas, and every mental act involved ideas from both faculties. Ideas in the intellect represented things outside the mind, such as 'a man, or a chimera, or even God', while ideas in the will were mental attitudes to what was represented by ideas in the intellect – attitudes of attraction, aversion, assertion or denial. Thus when an idea in the intellect, such as the idea of God, was combined with an idea in the will of assertion or denial, the result was a judgement, either to the effect that God exists, or to the effect that he does not. And when the idea of God was combined with an idea in the will of aversion or attraction, the result was a volition, consisting either in love or in hatred of God.[6]

Descartes put forward this analysis of thinking mainly because he thought that the distinction between intellect and will provided a way of reconciling the existence of human error with the existence of a benevolent and all-powerful God. In the first place, the analysis implied that error could not be attributed to the intellect. On their own ideas in the intellect could not be false, since they did not involve assertion or denial:

By the intellect alone (I do not assert or deny anything); I merely conceive ideas of the things about which I make judgments; and falsehood, properly so-called, is not to be found in it.[7]

Falsehood, properly so-called, or formal falsehood, is to be found only in judgments.[8]

Secondly, the analysis implied that error could not be attributed to the will on its own, since it was only in combination with ideas in the intellect that the will could produce volitions or judgements. It followed that the existence of human error did not mean that human beings had been created with a defect either in their will or in their intellect, so it did not mean that God was malevolent or incompetent.

Descartes applied his analysis of thinking to the sorts of processes involved in all the actions and experiences of everyday life. If a person moved his leg or felt hungry or looked at something, Descartes would have said he was using his ideas in order to form judgements or volitions. The lesson to be drawn from the investigation of knowledge of a piece of beeswax, for instance, was that 'what I used to think of myself as seeing with my eyes I really comprehend with my faculty of judging, which is in my mind'.[9] Thus Descartes's way of separating the mental and physical aspects of human beings involved treating thought as essential to many processes apart from abstract or lofty ratiocination – for example to 'manual' as well as to 'mental' work. This means that his attempt to disentangle mental and physical properties, though it deserves to be called dualism, was by no means a return to the Platonistic dualism of an intelligible world of perfect eternal ideas and a sensible world of particulars in chaotic flux.[10] Part of Descartes's dualism was the anti-Platonistic view that human activity and experience is always intellectual, or always involves thinking or ideas, even when it is based on senses or concerned with physical particulars, and even if it is apparently simple, unreflective or irrational.

Descartes's belief that all non-physical aspects of human beings could be reduced to thought is often concealed from modern readers because many of the words in which he expressed it have changed their meaning since his time.[11] Words like 'mind' and 'mental' have lost their austerely intellectualistic connotations, and have become much vaguer and wider in application. It has become common, even in careful philosophical discourse, to take physical sensations, such as toothache, as paradigm examples of 'mental' states[12]; and consequently it has become hard to see that Descartes was doing anything more than stating the obvious when he said that even physical sensation involves 'mental awareness'.[13] These changes in the meanings of words are due to the influence of a version of the theory of the mind that Descartes was opposed to – the pluralist theory that the mind has various attributes which cannot be reduced to thinking. This version of pluralism issued from the empiricist theory of mind, which implied that not only thoughts, but also things like pains might be ushered into the 'mind's presence chamber',[14] and it derived strength from its association with psychology, which came into being as a supposedly autonomous science in the eighteenth century. Psychologists thought their subject-matter was something called the mind, but they dealt with many human attributes – such as memory and sensation, emotions and feelings – which they did not see as reducible to thinking.

In the nineteenth century, the same pluralist concept of the mind was reaffirmed in a more purely philosophical context in the work of Husserl (1859–1938) and Frege (1848–1925), both of whom tried to rescue 'pure logic' from a supposed error which they called 'psychologism'. Psychologism, for them, was the view that logic should describe the actual structure and functioning of the human mind.[15] A byproduct of their anti-psychologism was the view that there are elements of the 'mental life' which cannot be explained in terms of thinking. Thus when Frege tried to defend logic from the 'corrupting incursion of psychology',[16] he divided the mind into two compartments, one containing mental imagery and the other thoughts (*Gedanken*). Thoughts were the subject-matter of logic, and they alone were true or false. Imagery was merely the 'colouring and shading' added to thoughts by 'poetic eloquence'.[17]

The pluralist way of defining the mind is based on the fact that if someone states in all sincerity that he is experiencing certain sensations, emotions or feelings, it seems impossible that his statement should be false. In general, it seems that people have unobstructed access to their own emotions, feelings and so on. Pluralism, then, is able to define a person's mind as that which he is immediately aware of, or of which he has certain and complete knowledge.[18] According to this definition, the fact that a person cannot have a physical sensation such as toothache without thinking he has one proves that toothaches are mental.

In a rather similar way, Descartes thought that the distinctive thing about a person's mental states is that it is impossible for him to doubt that he knows what they are like. Thus he said that the method of doubt 'prepares an easy way for accustoming our minds to separating themselves from the senses'.[19]

Thought was identical with mind, and thought was 'every-thing which happens within us in such a way that we are directly aware of it (*nobis consciis*), in so far as we are aware of it'.[20] Though Descartes did not make any precise separation between them, this definition of the mind in terms of in-dubitable knowledge is independent of the *cogito*. The *cogito* expresses the idea that it is impossible to doubt that one is thinking, whereas Descartes's definition of the mind expresses the idea that it is impossible to be in doubt about the identity of the thoughts one is having.

Descartes's way of defining the mind resembles that of the pluralists, in being based on the idea of certain knowledge. But the likeness is only superficial. He pointed out repeatedly that people can 'make mistakes in perceptions . . . which refer to certain parts of the body'.[21] So while he might not have had much objection to the pluralist view that one could not be mistaken about whether one is experiencing some physical sensation, like toothache, he would have argued that it was still possible to be mistaken about the specific character and location of one's sensations. For example, investigation might reveal that what I thought was toothache in my upper jaw is in fact in my lower jaw; or it might reveal that I am not suffering from toothache at all, but from an infection of the gums. So if I claimed that I was suffering from toothache in my upper jaw, my claim might conceivably turn out to be false, whereas if I restricted myself to claiming something about my thoughts, such as that I thought that there was something wrong with one of my teeth, my claim would be absolutely immune to doubt. Thus things like toothaches would not satisfy Descartes's definition of the mind. The only things which would do so were thoughts.

Even if it might make sense to entertain a general doubt as to whether one's thoughts were true, it would not make sense to doubt whether one knew what thoughts one was having. One's knowledge of the states of other things, and in particular of the states of one's body, was open to a kind of doubt which was completely inapplicable to one's knowledge of one's thoughts.

Moreover, states of the body could not themselves be thoughts, since they were not the sort of things which could meaningfully be described as true or false[22] or which could function as steps in syllogistic arguments.[23] According to Descartes, then, states which 'depend exclusively on the mind'[24] can be identified by the fact that people's knowledge of them leaves no room for doubt; and the only states which satisfy this criterion are 'nothing other than thinking'.[25] For Descartes my toothache is not a state of my mind any more than yours is. It is simply a state of my tooth.

Descartes's view that insofar as they are not states of the body, sensations are nothing but thoughts is likely to strike modern readers as extremely narrow and restrictive. It seems to ignore completely what Frege called the 'imagery' which accompanies thoughts.

Descartes would have said that when I have an itch in my fingers, I am making a judgement about them; and he would have said that the same judgement might have been made even by a person whose hand had been amputated,[26] or even, conceivably, by a person who did not have a body at all. Maurice Merleau-Ponty, the most important modern critic of Descartes's account of the mind, objects to the 'intellectualism' of this analysis, pointing out that 'experiencing an amputated arm as present, or a sick arm as absent, is not an experience of the same order as "I think that ...".'[27] It seems obvious that there is some truth in this objection: the majority of human experiences are not pondered upon in an abstracted, passive way, and it is often impossible to capture the finer features of experience in the coarse net of clumsy everyday words. This seems even more obvious when one considers experiences like being half-conscious of an itch in one's fingers, or conjuring up the nebulous image of the face of a long-lost friend, or being tormented by an incoherent and senseless dream. So it seems that Descartes's attempt to reduce such things to thinking is crude, insensitive and inept. From this point of view, it is easy to criticize Descartes as someone who was so preoccupied with intellectual matters and with arid argumentation about cold and inhuman subjects like algebra, refraction and problems of scientific method that he forgot what real, lived, human experience was like.

Such criticisms of Descartes's analysis of sensation beg the question. They rely on the assumption that there are mental attributes – like 'imagery' – which cannot be reduced to thoughts, and on the resulting habit of applying the word 'thinking' only to those elements of the mental life which are ponderous, rational, conscious and closely linked to verbal expression.[28] But Descartes would not have restricted the application of the word 'thinking' so narrowly. He was prepared to acknowledge the existence of non-verbal ways of expressing thoughts: he regarded the use of diagrams as indispensable in scientific and mathematical thinking, and he would have regarded manual work, music, dancing and gesturing as expressions of thinking too. He could also have admitted that a person's thinking might be so rich, complex and nuanced that it was practically impossible to express it. In saying such things, Descartes would not have been idly flouting the normal use of the word 'thinking'. He would have been stating the very significant thesis that human action and perception are more intellectual than they seem, in that they always involve thinking, ideas or mind; and hence that they are built on structures not wholly different from those involved in what the Platonistic theory would call intellectual knowledge.

Descartes's account of mind led him into a curious theological unorthodoxy. Like most other Christians, he thought it was possible for individual souls to exist independently of bodies (see below, pp.116-17). The orthodox view of this possibility, expressed by Aquinas, was that it involved having no knowledge of the sensible world.[29] It was partly for this reason that Christians attached such importance to the doctrine that all disembodied souls would at some time in the future be reunited with their bodies; for otherwise, they would be permanently deprived of sensory knowledge. Descartes's account of mind allowed this difficult doctrine to be set aside, since it implied that there was no limit to what a disembodied soul might experience. The question is whether Descartes can legitimately have meant anything by talking about disembodied souls.

[10]

Dualism and Materialism

Descartes's reductionist physical theory seemed to threaten human values with obliteration by the mechanical laws of an indifferent universe. Part of his response to this threat was his dualism of mental and physical properties, which implied that since human beings had minds, they were more than mere parts of an all-engulfing physical universe. But it has seemed to many of Descartes's readers that his solution created more problems than it solved. If mental and physical properties are totally different, then the interaction of mind and body seems to be completely mysterious.[1] The standard objection to his dualism is that, in saying both that the mind is not a physical thing and that it influences and is influenced by physical things, he was contradicting himself.

Before the seventeenth century, this objection would not even have appeared to have any validity. The possibility of mind affecting body would not have seemed any more mysterious than the possibility of, say, weather affecting crops. This situation changed when the new, reductionist physics promised a complete account of the physical world in terms of matter and motion. It then became possible to raise a relatively precise problem – whether something not itself subject to the laws of physics could influence the motions of physical particles. Descartes's account of the interaction of mind and body involved the idea that thinking is a process which occurs inside people's pineal glands, and that it affects and is affected by the movements of the gland. He was convinced, however, that the states of a person's body – of his arms, legs, lips and tongue, and of the animal spirits in his brain and indeed of his pineal gland – were completely reducible to the fundamental properties of matter. The standard objection to his view of the mind as non-physical seems to be that, given a reductionist approach to the states of the human body, the hypothesis that non-physical processes are taking place inside the pineal gland is completely useless: for even if non-physical processes did

---

A soul hung up as 'twere, in Chains
Of nerves and Arteries and Veins . . .

Andrew Marvell[2]

---

occur they would not make any difference to the purely physical system which is the human body. The mind would be stranded and powerless, an absurd and useless appendage to the human body.

Descartes's fixation on the pineal gland – which is now known to be a vestigial eye, and to have no function – is rather ridiculous; but his view of the possibility of interaction between mind and body is neither irrational nor inconsistent with his scientific outlook. It would only have been so if, in addition to being reductionist, his physical theory had been determinist. A determinist physical theory would say that given the physical state of the universe at any one time, its physical state at absolutely any other time is determined down to the last detail. It is most unlikely that any such theory is true, but if it were then it would indeed be silly to suppose that thinking could make any difference to the movements of people's bodies.[3] For scientific purposes even the movements of my lips and tongue to form words would be able to be explained without reference to my thoughts or intentions. In this case, any theory which referred to thought or consciousness would be vulnerable to the standard objection to Descartes's dualism.

Descartes, however, could not possibly have thought that his physical theory was determinist. At the heart of it there was a vague, indeed unworkable, definition of momentum (see above, pp. 55–57), and this made it very obvious that even given all the movements in the universe at any one moment, Cartesian physics left open countless possibilities as to what movements could take place at any other time. According to Leibniz, Descartes deliberately exploited the indeterminacy in his physical theory in order to explain how thought can have effects on the physical world. Leibniz drew attention to the fact that while Descartes's physical theory says that the amount of motion in a closed system cannot change, it assumes that this quantity can be evaluated without reference to direction. So, according to Leibniz, it was easy for Descartes to explain how the mind could affect the motion of the animal spirits without being subject to the laws of nature: he could claim that it affected the direction of their motion but not the quantity of it. However, as Leibniz also pointed out, subsequent developments in physical theory subjected direction as well as quantity of movement to laws of nature, and even though this did not make physical theory completely determinist, it eliminated the particular solution to the problem of interaction which Leibniz attributed to Descartes.[4]

The rejection of Descartes's account of how immaterial processes in the pineal gland might affect physical processes in the brain did not lead to the complete abandonment of his concept of the soul. Thinkers like La Mettrie (1709–51), Helvétius (1715–51) and Holbach (1723–89), as well as taking over Locke's empiricist theory of mind, took over Descartes's reductionist ideal for physics, and his conception of the soul as a homunculus in the middle of the nervous system. They thought, however, that it was only because of sentimentality, or perhaps even dishonesty, that Descartes had stopped short of saying that thinking was reducible to the fundamental properties of matter. Thus they rejected Descartes's dualism, while retaining his homunculus account of the soul or mind. The young Marx called them 'Cartesian materialists'.[5]

The development of classical physics was associated with a tendency to add items like gravity to Descartes's list of the

It would be very singular that all nature and all the stars should obey eternal laws and that there should be one little animal, five feet tall, which, despite these laws, could always act as suited its caprice.

Voltaire[6]

universal properties of matter (see above, pp. 54-55). On the whole, the Cartesian materialists thought they could explain the nature of mind simply by adding further items like thought, memory and sensation to the list.[7] Their theory had valuable byproducts, because it acted as a stimulus for research into the apparently non-mechanical attributes of animal tissues, such as irritability.[8] It also had important corollaries in other fields, being associated with atheism and political radicalism, and with the idea that habits of thought depend on social and natural environment. But as a theory about the nature of mind, it was extremely inadequate. It implied that it might make sense to attribute thoughts to any piece of matter, regardless of its history and its setting: to a candle, a strand of hair, a star, a cloud or a puddle. It tried to make problems about the nature of mind disappear simply by applying the word 'physical' to thought.

Descartes was forced to confront this sort of materialism because a speculative statement of it was published in 1647 by one of the early champions of Cartesian physics, Henri Le Roy (1598-1679) of the University of Utrecht.[9] Le Roy had conjectured that thinking might be a fundamental property, or 'mode', of matter[10]; and Descartes's impatient reply was that 'the mind can be comprehended by us apart from matter, and therefore is not a mode of matter'.[11] This was a reference to the use of the method of doubt for 'separating the mind from the body'. Descartes's argument for his dualism, or against materialism, was that if, for some reason, one doubted the existence of physical things, one would be bound to doubt the existence of the modes of matter, such as extension, shape and movement, and that this would not mean one had to doubt the existence of thoughts. It followed that mental properties were not a type of physical properties.

Descartes's argument against materialism expresses an important and valid insight into the difference between the specification of a thought and reductive scientific explanations of physical phenomena. Specifying a thought is specifying what can be called a structural property. The peculiarity of structural properties is that one and the same structural property can be 'encoded' or 'embodied' in an infinite number of physical forms: for example, in a composer's brain, in his manuscript, in a printed score, in the sound-waves in a concert hall, in the grooves of a gramophone record, in a magnetic tape, in radio-waves and so on.[12] They are therefore amongst the properties which, unlike, say, redness or luminosity, could not possibly be given a reductive definition in terms of the fundamental properties of matter. Reductive descriptions of the relevant features of the brain, the manuscript, the magnetic tape and so on would not provide one with a specification of the structural properties which they have in common.[13] Therefore structural properties are not reducible to the fundamental properties of matter – at least not in the sense of 'reduction' which characterizes the classical, Cartesian ideal of scientific explanation.

So Descartes was right in his opposition to the view that thinking can be explained by a reductive physical science. The Cartesian materialists, unlike Descartes, overestimated the power and scope of Cartesian and post-Cartesian physics. In denying that there were any properties which could not be explained in its terms, they were in effect denying the existence of structural properties, and thereby denying the existence of thought.

It is past controversy, that we have in us something that thinks.

Locke[14]

For at least two centuries, scientists tended to be so over-awed by the reductionist ideal of scientific explanation that it more or less defined their concept of science. Consequently they paid very little attention to structural properties. Recently, however, psychologists and linguists of certain schools, anthropologists and workers in computer science and artificial intelligence have deliberately set out to investigate structural properties without bothering about the old ideal reducing them to the fundamental properties of matter. Of course, scientists in these fields tend to think of themselves as materialists; but this only shows that the word 'materialism' has acquired a new meaning. The same new meaning can be found in the works of certain modern philosophers who think of themselves as materialists even though they deny that mental states are reducible to physical ones.[15] These modern materialists either state, or silently assume, that the ideal of reductive physical explanation cannot be applied to thinking, and this means that their position has more in common with Cartesian dualism than with Cartesian materialism.

The phrase 'Cartesian dualism' (often shortened to 'Cartesianism' or 'dualism') has been widely used as a blanket term for the theories of mind which Ryle and Wittgenstein attacked. One main target of their attacks was what Ryle called 'Descartes's Myth' and the 'dogma of the Ghost in the Machine',[16] which is the view that apart from their ordinary, observable lives, people lead an inner, mental life known only to themselves. This 'dogma' implied that facts about a person's mind were only externally[17] related to socially observable facts; and it followed that the individual's mind was a private world, to which only he had access, and which was a complete world in itself in the sense that it could be described exhaustively without reference to anything outside it. The main historical proponents of such views were the empiricists, and in particular the Cartesian materialists. But the Cartesian materialists did not think there was anything ghostly about the mind; in fact they were sure that there was nothing to it but states of the animal spirits in the middle of people's heads, which, they thought, could be identified without any reference to things outside, and therefore without reference to anything that was socially observable. Thus, in spite of Ryle's references to 'ghosts', one of the main targets of his arguments is Cartesian materialism. His arguments are attacks on the idea that the mind is hidden inside the body, and they have no particular relevance to Cartesian dualism, which is perfectly compatible with the view that all mental states are internally related to states which are socially observable.

It is true that Descartes thought of the mind as a sort of homunculus inside the body. He had adopted this view in his early writings, before working out his dualism; and he never altogether abandoned it. He continued to think, for example, that the mind 'receives impressions . . . only from the brain, or even from one of its smallest parts'.[18] On the other hand, he did slightly modify his account:

Nature also teaches me by the sensations of pain, hunger, thirst, etc., that I am not only lodged in my body like a pilot in a ship, but that I am very closely united to it and (so to speak) so intermingled with it that I seem to compose with it one whole. For if that were not the case, if my body was hurt, I, who am merely a thinking thing, should not feel pain, for I should perceive this wound by the understanding only, just as a sailor perceives by sight when there is some damage done to his ship.[19]

This is obviously an unsatisfactory piece of reasoning. It is based on the quite extraordinary idea that a person cannot care about a physical object unless his mind is spatially mingled with it. The source of the confusion is that Descartes was trying to weld together two positions – dualism and the homunculus concept of the mind or soul – which are completely independent of each other. In fact, particularly in the light of his identification of matter with space (see above, pp. 51-52) they are scarcely compatible.

Thus, in Descartes's late philosophy there was a tension between his dualism and the homunculus theory from which it developed; and it is therefore a mistake to suppose that there is a unified position, or a set of mutually supporting positions, in the philosophy of mind, which can be labelled 'Cartesianism'. For Descartes, however, the two doctrines appeared to be inseparable, being proved together by the method of doubt. This contradiction is a very fundamental feature of his late philosophy, and it infects every department of it with ambiguity. In his search for certain knowledge, Descartes the dualist retreated into a world of thoughts, while Descartes the homunculus theorist retreated into his pineal gland. When he reflected on the meaning of this retreat, part of him wondered whether there were any objects corresponding to ideas; but another part wondered whether he was the only individual in the world. The combination or superimposition of these two approaches had profound and ramified implications for Descartes's views about the soul.

[11]

The Immortal Soul

Primitive theories of the soul treat it as a sort of physical substance or ectoplasm.[1] According to Frazer, 'the savage thinks of [the soul] as a concrete material thing of a definite bulk, capable of being seen and handled, kept in a box or jar, and liable to be bruised, fractured, or smashed in pieces'.[2] A similar view was current amongst the ancient Greeks. Homer thought of the *psyche* or *thumos* as something which escaped from the human body at death, either through the mouth or through wounds,[3] and Democritus said it was a 'body within a body', distinguished by the spherical shape, fineness and mobility of its parts.[4] Similarly, the ancient Egyptians regarded the inner spirit of man, Ka, as a physical body requiring food and drink.[5] This concept of the soul as ectoplasm was taken over by the early Christians. For example, Tertullian (165–220)

That man should be a thing for immortal souls to sieve through!

Herman Melville[6]

---

had a dream which convinced him that the soul was 'soft, transparent, and of an ethereal colour'.[7] Descartes himself, sensitive to the histories of various words for the soul, claimed that when he was young he had thought that the soul was 'like a kind of wind, fire, or ether'.[8] However, his physical theory implied that the properties of any material thing were reducible to the universal properties of matter, and this destroyed the appeal of the ectoplasmic concept of the soul. If the soul was a physical thing, then from the point of view of Cartesian physics there could be no justification for thinking of it as having a unique place in the universe.

Christian theory of Descartes's time offered an alternative approach to the problem. In the Middle Ages scholastic

Christian thinkers had taken over an Aristotelian concept of the soul. According to them the soul was a 'substantial form' which 'informed' matter. This implied that the soul was dependent on matter, but could not be identified with it. The scholastics did not take this to mean that the soul was always embodied; but they did think that every soul must sometimes be associated with a body. Thus Aquinas asserted that 'the soul will not be for ever without the body' and that 'the immortality of the soul seems to demand the future resurrection of bodies'.[9]

In the seventeenth century, the notion of substantial forms in general was subject to powerful criticisms, particularly from Descartes (see above, p. 42). Its application to the soul was particularly problematic, for two reasons. First, if the body disintegrated between death and resurrection, it was hard to see how the soul which depended on it could continue to exist.[10] Second, the notion of bodily resurrection presented curious logistical problems. What would happen, for instance, if a dead man's body entered a natural cycle and became the food and then part of the body of another man? Whose body would the piece of matter belong to on Resurrection Day? Thus both the traditional ways of conceiving of the soul – as ectoplasm and as substantial form – were unacceptable to Descartes.

It would have been understandable if Descartes had drawn the conclusion that the notion of the soul ought to be completely abandoned. In fact, however, he thought he could salvage the notion of the soul and rebuild it on a fully scientific basis. He believed that, apart from angels and God, the only things which could think, or which had minds, were human beings. He never presented any good reasons for this opinion, however.[11] It would not be absurd to attribute minds, as he conceived them, to animals and machines, and to be a dualist about these as well as about human beings. But in conjunction with his dualism of mind and matter (see above, p. 91), and his identification of the soul with the mind (see above, p. 76), the opinion that machines and animals could not have minds enabled Descartes to offer Christian theory a new concept of the soul. The human soul, according to Descartes, was something

> whose entire nature or essence is simply to think, and which needs no space to exist in, and does not depend on any material thing. Thus this me, that is to say this soul by which I am what I am, is altogether distinct from the body; it is more easily known, and it would be exactly what it is even if the body had never existed.[12]

Descartes tried to prove the correctness of this new concept of the soul by means of an argument which includes both the grounds of his dualism of mind and matter and the grounds of his idealist identification of the soul with the mind. The argument has two stages. The first stage is an attempt to prove that idealism might conceivably be true. (I am using the word 'idealism' in a rather archaic eighteenth-century sense to mean the view that nothing exists except thinking.) Descartes did not really give an argument for the conceivability of idealism: he simply asserted it. He asserted, in effect, that it is possible to specify any thought without presupposing anything at all about matter and its modes, and without even presupposing that matter exists. Clearly, this assertion echoes his argument for dualism, which says that it is possible to specify a thought without presupposing anything in particular about matter; but equally clearly, it goes beyond it and is far more dubious. At the same time, it is extremely difficult to refute.

Idealism can only be refuted by a demonstration that the existence of thoughts entails the existence of other things. The most promising way of trying to provide such a demonstration is to take examples of thoughts which seem particularly dependent on having a body, like thoughts laden with sexual desire or bodily distress. If having such thoughts presupposes having a body, then their existence disproves idealism. But a tenacious idealist could say that while having such thoughts presupposes believing that one has a body, it does not presuppose actually having one.

Another approach is to take examples of thoughts which are

highly culture-specific. If I think I have been short-changed in a shop, for instance, then my thoughts could not be specified without mention of institutions like money and shops. And if having such thoughts presupposes the existence of such a setting, idealism must be false. But once again it is easy for the idealist to defend himself. He can claim that the only setting necessary for a person to be able to think he has been short-changed is that he should believe that institutions like shops and money exist; and this belief might be false.

A more powerful argument against idealism is that people must be able to distinguish between their thoughts on the one hand and the objects which their thoughts are about on the other. Otherwise, according to the argument, people would not be able to make sense of their experience at all, because they would not be able to understand the possibility of their thoughts being true or false. But once again, a tenacious idealist would be able to defend himself. He could simply say that he accepted the conclusion that people cannot make sense of their experience. At this point, attempts to disprove the conceivability of idealism seem to run into the ground.[13]

But it is possible to adopt another and more damaging line of attack on idealism. The poverty of idealism is that it is unable to give any explanation of the nature of thinking. In particular, it cannot give any account of how people identify thoughts and distinguish between them. For instance, it cannot explain how people can distinguish between the thought of money and the thought of, say, a rainbow. Instead, it has to take this as a brute fact or an inexplicable mystery. In the archaic sense in which I have been using the word 'idealism', then, idealism is hardly worth stating or attacking; and Descartes did not really give any reason for taking it seriously.

But when Descartes raised the question of the conceivability of idealism in the early parts of the *Meditations*, he was only using it as an artificial device; and in the later parts of the *Meditations* he tried to show that idealism does not in fact make sense (see below, p. 136). This procedure is sometimes referred to as the 'Cartesian paradox'[14]; but it is less paradoxical than it seems. The sort of sense Descartes wanted to attribute to idealism was the sort of twilight sense which in time fades into total obscurity.[15] It may be doubted whether he succeeded in giving it even this much sense, but it is still worth looking at his attempt to use the discussion of it to illuminate the nature of the human soul.

When he was satisfied that he had demonstrated that idealism is conceivable, Descartes asserted that even if someone believed in idealism he would have no reason to doubt the existence of his soul. If this step could be taken, he thought, the validity of his concept of the soul would be proved. But the step cannot be taken. The trouble with Descartes's argument is not that it depends on the method of doubt; nor that it depends on the dubious hypothesis that idealism is conceivable. It is that the assertion that idealism does not cast doubt on the existence of the soul is demonstrably false, at least on any orthodox conception of the soul. Although Descartes did not intend it to, his concept of the soul contradicted orthodox Christian views about the individuality of souls.

Orthodox Christians believe that to each living human body there corresponds exactly one soul. For example, the supposition that the sad middle-aged philosopher lying on his deathbed in Sweden in 1650 might have a different soul from that of the arrogant young mathematician who captivated his Paris audience in 1628 would not make sense to them. They would be certain that the same soul, that of René Descartes, was present on both occasions. His thoughts might have changed or contradicted each other, but he would still have had one and the same soul throughout his life; and someone else might have had thoughts identical with his, but Descartes and the other person would not have had one and the same soul. This is reflected in the English idioms in which a person can be said to be 'in two minds', but not 'in two souls'; or to 'change his mind', but not to 'change his soul'; and where several people can be said to be 'of one mind', but not 'of one soul'. Descartes's concept of the soul, however, involving as it did the identification of the soul with the mind, was incompatible with the orthodox view of the individuality of souls. Though Descartes did not realize it, his concept of the soul cast doubt on the assumption that there is exactly one soul corresponding to each living human body.

Leibniz developed Descartes's concept of the soul in a way which avoided this clash with orthodox assumptions. He argued that different human beings are bound to see the world from different points of view,[16] and that as a consequence their minds are bound to be different. But this development of Descartes's concept of the soul is really a negation of it. It only supports the attempt to explain the identity or individuality of souls in terms of the identity of minds by saying that the identity of minds depends on the identity of bodies. Leibniz was therefore right to see himself as an opponent of the Cartesian view of the soul, which he thought was advocated by 'the majority of moderns'. In opposition to it, he asserted that 'all minds (*génies*) and souls ... are always joined to some body'.[17]

Spinoza also took over Descartes's concept of the soul. But unlike Leibniz he did not modify it, and he followed it through with remarkable consistency to its logical conclusion: the rejection of orthodox ideas about the individuality of souls. According to Spinoza, if you and I had all the same thoughts then we would both have the same soul.[18] Moreover, if our minds contained nothing but complete scientific knowledge of the universe – which Spinoza thought was provided by Cartesian physics – our souls would be identical not only with each other's, but also with God's. For Spinoza, then, the acquisition of scientific knowledge meant the complete annihilation of the individual soul. Spinoza is not the only philosopher to have departed from the view that there must be just one soul associated with each living human body. In Buddhist philosophy, for example, the orthodox Christian notion of the soul would be treated as an individualistic illusion. The same attitude is to be found in an unorthodox Christian

theory known as Averroism.[19] Equally, the belief that one man
can have several souls is a recurrent theme of primitive philo-
sophies.[20] It can be argued that all these notions of the soul are
incoherent, on the ground that it is necessary to have a conception of oneself as one individual amongst others in order to
make sense of one's experience of the world and of other
people, and of other people's experience of the world. But
whether this argument is valid or not, it is clear that Descartes
himself had no intention of casting doubt on orthodox Christian
views of the individuality of souls – though one of his contemporaries did accuse him of Averroism.[21] Descartes thought his
concept of the soul was simply a clarification or reconstruction
of the orthodox notion; and in this opinion he was mistaken.

Descartes was confident that his concept of the soul laid a
completely firm basis for the orthodox Christian theory and
that Christian apologists ought to be grateful to him.[22] His
achievement, as he saw it, was that he had worked out an
alternative both to thinking of the soul as a physical thing
composed of ectoplasm, and to thinking of it as a substantial
form. He thought he had shown that it was a pure, non-
physical substance. In Descartes's time the word 'substance' was
used mainly to mean particular individual things, like a chair
or a man or an angel, or rather the aspect of them that abides
when their properties change; it was used especially to mean
spatio-temporal particulars. (It still has this meaning in the
technical language of philosophy.) Sometimes this concept of
substance was explained by comparing the substance to a naked
body and its changing properties to clothes. And sometimes
this underlying body came to be thought of as completely
propertiless. All the properties associated with a thing would
then be compared with clothes, and it became very mysterious
what, if anything, this underlying body was.

Descartes was critical of the 'underlying body' analogy (see
above, pp. 79-80). He was particularly opposed to the idea that
in itself a substance had no properties. For instance, he thought
that the substance of physical things could be identified with

the property of extension. For the purposes of his physical theory, then, his concept of substance did not need to have any connotations of individuality. When he discussed the application of the notion to the piece of beeswax, he was really interested in the properties of 'wax in general', rather than in the individuality of this particular piece.[23] His use of the word 'substance' in this context was therefore very close to its modern use to mean mass chemicals (e.g. 'poisonous substance'). But Descartes thought all the chemical principles were reducible to one, namely extension, and therefore that 'there is only one physical substance'.[24]

But why did Descartes wish to extend the notion of substance to thought? Why did he not say that all substance is physical, but that it sometimes has irreducible mental properties? The answer is that he took his reductionist ideal for physics as providing a definition of the physical world: he refused to regard anything as physical if it could not be explained by his physics. It is for this reason that he was convinced that substantial forms, which were by definition irreducible, had to be expelled from physics. But of course there was one thing which he considered to be irreducible: thinking. It was therefore natural for him to call thought itself a substance. Sometimes Descartes wrote as though he believed that thought was a substance in the same sense as extension. 'We may consider thought and extension as constituting the natures of intelligent and physical substance; but then they must not be considered as anything apart from the very substances that think and are extended, i.e. as mind and matter.'[25] But if thinking substance is identified with thought in general, then it is obviously impossible to explain the individuality of souls in terms of thought. In this sense, there might be only one mental substance, just as there was only one physical substance. For this reason Descartes had to develop a rather different notion of substance.[26] Substances, in this sense, had a pure but inexplicable individuality. Descartes told Burman: 'Besides the attribute which specifies a substance, we must recognise the substance itself which supports the attribute.

For instance, the soul, being a thinking thing, is, in addition to thought, a substance which thinks.'[27] Descartes, normally extremely confident about the power of the human mind (especially his own), seems to be saying that a complete account of the attribute of thinking would not be a complete account of thinking substance, because thinking substance is something 'in addition to thought'.[28] He had to say this because his concept of the soul would otherwise have conflicted very obviously with orthodox ideas about the individuality of souls. The idea of an unknowable thinking substance apart from the attribute of thinking enabled him to say that 'Even if all the properties (*accidents*) of the mind change . . . it does not become another mind.'[29]

It is impossible to see any sense in Descartes's notion of individual mental substances. On the one hand he wanted to talk about thinking substance, and on the other hand he thought that a specification of its properties does not count as talking about it. But talking about something cannot possibly be anything but trying to specify its properties, so Descartes's conception of thinking substance was useless.

Descartes thought his concept of the soul provided a new and easy way of proving various old Christian doctrines, or something quite like them. The word 'substance' meant, according to Descartes, 'a thing which so exists that it needs no other thing in order to exist',[30] so if the soul or mind was a substance, it would follow that souls or minds could exist quite independently of bodies. So Descartes thought he had proved the possibility of souls being disembodied, and not just temporarily, as Aquinas had envisaged, but forever.

Descartes also thought that his concept of the soul as a substance proved that souls were indestructible, and hence supported the traditional Christian belief in immortality. But he never explained the point satisfactorily. He promised an explanation in the subtitle of the first edition of the *Meditations*; but the explanation was not to be found in the *Meditations* themselves, but only in the synopsis of them, which was written just as the work was going to press.[31] The demonstration was based on an analogy with the conservation principles of Cartesian physics.

> ... The premisses from which the immortality of the mind *(mentis, âme)* can be deduced, depend on the explanation of the whole of physics. First it must be known that in general every substance, that is everything created by God, is of its nature incorruptible, and can only become nothing if this same God decides to withdraw his (usual) support. Secondly it must be realised that body taken generally is a substance: this is why it too cannot perish; whereas the human body, to the extent that it differs from other bodies, is nothing but a combination *(conflatum, formé et composé)* of limbs and other similar properties *(accidentibus, accidents)*. The human soul *(mentem, âme)*, in contrast, does not consist of properties *(accidentibus, accidents)* in this way, but is a pure substance ... It follows that a particular body can easily perish, whereas the mind *(mentem, esprit)*, (or the human soul (I do not distinguish the two)) is by its very nature immortal.[32]

This is an extraordinarily feeble argument. First, Descartes gives no reason for supposing that mental substance is analogous to physical substance. Second, he gives no reason for comparing individual souls or minds with 'body taken generally' rather than with individual bodies. It is not surprising, therefore, that the reference to a proof of immortality was dropped from the title-page of the second edition of the *Meditations*.

[12]

Freedom and Action

Descartes sometimes expressed his belief that the soul is the same as the mind by saying that the essence of a person is thinking. This suggests that his statements about the soul are in part similar to, say, Shaw's statements about the essence of Ibsenism, and that they are simply meant to single out the features which make human beings human. Descartes's opinion was that 'the most important thing is the mind'.[1]

This view of the soul must be seen in the context of a general theory of actions and passions. The basis of the concepts of action and passion is fairly simple.[2] In general, things are in a state of action, or active, when they are expressing or 'actualizing' their own nature or essence; but when they behave in a way which is not determined by their own essence, they are passive.[3] When a sapling forces its way up through concrete, the sapling is behaving in a way which is natural for it, in that it is on its way to becoming a tree, while the concrete is simply being acted on by the sapling; the sapling is active and the concrete is passive.

Questions about action and passion played an important part in the establishment of classical physics. Traditional Aristotelian theory had stated that it was in the nature of inanimate heavy objects to remain stationary as long as they were in their natural place on the surface of the earth. It followed that for such bodies movement was a passion, not an action. If an ox was dragging a cart across a plain, then the moment it stopped pulling the cart would stop moving. According to the Aristotelians, this was because it was in the nature of things like carts to be stationary when in this position. But this way of looking at motion led into difficulties. For example, it made it puzzling that the cart might carry on moving for a while even after the ox had stopped pulling it. Descartes's greatest contribution to the overthrow of Aristotelian physics was that, extending Galileo's work, he constructed a new way of distinguishing which movements of physical objects were natural, and which were not. According to Descartes, what was natural for a heavy object on the surface of the earth (and equally, for any physical object in the entire universe) was not that it should be stationary but that it should maintain uniform movement in a straight line. It was not its continued movement, but its failure to move uniformly in a straight line for ever which was unnatural. In other words, the continued movement of the cart did not have to be explained as a passion due to forces impressed on the cart from outside. The third Law of Nature in *The World* states this principle as follows:

> When a body is moving, even though it will usually be taking a curved path . . . nevertheless all the particular bits of the body have a tendency to continue their motion in a straight line. Thus their action, that is to say the inclination they have to move themselves, is different from their movement.[4]

Descartes's view that the essence of a person is thinking was, in part, a similar attempt to provide a way of distinguishing what is natural from what is not.

The classification of human behaviour into actions and passions presupposes a conception of the nature or essence of human beings. (In this connection, the word 'passions' does not have its usual connotations of agitation or emotion.)[5] One such conception is that the essential attributes of a person are amongst those which he acquires in the course of his life, rather than those he was born with. On this conception, if a person's good looks, or irritable temper, or intellectual powers are regarded as inborn characteristics, then what flows from these is something the person cannot help; it is not his action, but his passion.

Descartes's identification of the soul with the mind, or his view that a person's essence is thinking, provides an alternative way of dividing a person's behaviour into actions and passions.

It implies that a person is active when his behaviour is an expression of his thought, and that otherwise he is passive. 'The only things which should be counted as human actions are those which depend on reason,' he said.[6] A person whose behaviour issued from his thought was active; a person whose behaviour issued from anything else was passive.

Descartes equated activity with freedom and passivity with bondage. Thus he did not think, as some people have done, that free human behaviour is undetermined or unrestrained or uncontrolled like free fall or a free market. On the contrary, he thought that free human behaviour was completely controlled. A person's behaviour was free if it was controlled by his own nature or essence as a thinking being. Using scholastic terminology, Descartes said that human freedom, at least in its highest form, was 'liberty of spontaneity', and not 'liberty of indifference'.[7] Thus his identification of soul and mind implied

---

Thought constitutes the greatness of man . . . In space, the universe encompasses me and swallows me up like an atom; by thought, I comprehend the world.

Pascal[8]

---

that human behaviour is not really free unless it expresses thought.

Ethical appraisals of people are always based on what they do rather than what is done to them; on what they are responsible for, rather than on what they cannot help; in other words on their actions rather than on their passions. The most important corollary of Descartes's view of the human soul is that an ethical appraisal of a person presupposes that his behaviour is in some way an expression of thought.[9] And whether this corollary is true or false, it is an expression of a common sense which is almost universal, at least in cultures influenced by Christianity.[10]

Descartes's view of the soul is often attacked for its supposedly ascetic or Puritanical ethical implications. But such criticisms are nearly always based on misunderstandings. D. H. Lawrence tried to criticize Descartes's view when he made the odd announcement that 'My sex is me as my mind is me.'[11] But Lawrence did not really mean that people should identify themselves with sex as opposed to thought; he was only calling for people to regard sexual thoughts, or sexual consciousness, as essential to human nature,[12] and this in itself is not incompatible with Descartes's identification of the soul with the mind. Similarly, when Norman O. Brown claims that 'the true essence of man consists not, as Descartes maintained, in thinking, but in desiring'[13] he simply misunderstands Descartes; for Descartes included desires, or volitions, amongst thoughts.[14] Thinking, according to Descartes, was involved even in the most carnal and lascivious human activity.

Descartes's account of human actions and passions was infected with ambiguity by the tension between his homunculus account of the soul and his dualism of mental and physical properties (see above, pp. 106-107). In spite of his dualism, many of Descartes's remarks about the human mind were based on physiology, almost as though he regarded thinking as a physical process. The tension is particularly great in Descartes's last book, *The Passions of the Soul*, which was written for Princess Elizabeth, and published, in French, in 1649. The only way to understand the book is to treat it as containing two quite different theories of human actions and passions, one corresponding to each tendency of Descartes's account.

Descartes thought of the soul as something which attempts to control the movements of the body while remaining cooped up in the pineal gland at the centre of the nervous system; and this provided him with a simple way of accounting for the difference between human actions and passions. Human action, or behaviour which expressed thought, was behaviour whose cause could be traced back through the nervous system to the pineal gland. On the other hand:

Those of our movements to which our will does not contribute (such as much of our breathing, walking, eating, and other actions which we have in common with animals) depend only on the structure of our members and the route which the animal spirits, excited by the heat of the heart, naturally take in the brain, nerves and muscles, just as the movements of a watch are produced solely by the force of its springs and the shape of its wheels.[15]

This purely mechanical behaviour – or 'reflex' behaviour as it might be called – was identified with a person's passions. Descartes's explanation of such behaviour has remarkable parallels with modern behaviourist theories of conditioning.[16] For instance, he claimed that if a person associates certain things with danger, then his brain automatically prepares him for flight when these things are imagined or perceived.[17] If the person fled as a result, his flight would be mechanical and not free; it would be a passion rather than an action.

Descartes thought that his physiological theories showed how the traditional ethical ideal of conquering one's passions ought to be approached. If possible, one should train one's nervous system; and the way to do this could be learned from the way dogs are trained for hunting.[18] But sometimes there might be no way of preventing one's nervous system from being thrown into chaotic agitation. 'The most the will can do while this agitation is in full force is not to consent to effects, and to restrain some of the movements to which it disposes the body. For instance, if anger makes us raise our hands to strike, our will can usually hold it back.'[19] Descartes seems to have thought that in states of extreme agitation the relation of a person to his body resembles that of a rider to a horse which has gone berserk; and his main advice to the rider seems to be that he ought to hold on tight. This view of the distinction between human action and passion seems, amongst other things, to reinstate Puritanism or asceticism: it seems to reduce morality to a struggle between the flesh and the spirit.

But Descartes superimposed on this theory of the passions another and very different one. Though he did not notice the incongruence, his other theory does not identify the distinction between human actions and passions with the distinction between behaviour caused by the soul or mind and behaviour caused by the body. Instead, it applies the distinction only to states of the mind, or thoughts. Thoughts were classified as actions if they expressed the thinker's nature as a thinking being; and if they were a response to anything else, they were classified as passions. This 'anything else' included not only one's own body but also things and people outside it: thus Descartes called all perceptions of external objects passions.[20] On the dualist account of the passions, then, the struggle against the passions was not necessarily a struggle against the flesh.[21]

Descartes's attempt to marry two incompatible accounts of human action and passion made his notion of a person's essence as a thinking being ambiguous. On the homunculus interpretation, a person's essence would be constituted by whatever thoughts he happened to be having, so that he could be considered as active whenever the causes of his movements could be traced back to his pineal gland. But the dualist interpretation required a distinction between thoughts which expressed a person's essential nature, and thoughts which did not; it required the problematic notion of an inner self.

[13]

The Inner Self

In the sixteenth and seventeenth centuries, as capitalism began to establish itself in Europe, new forms of consciousness and new theories of human nature came into being. It became normal for people to think of themselves as equal competitors in a commodity market, rather than as having a natural place in a God-given social hierarchy. Regardless of rank, people increasingly came to 'recognise in each other the rights of private proprietors'.[1] Even the labouring poor were proprietors, with a native endowment of property in the form of their ability to work, or labour power. As Locke said, 'Every man has a *Property* in his own *Person* ... The *Labour* of his Body, and the *Work* of his Hands, we may say, are properly his.'[2] Individuals were connected with a social framework only by means of commodities, and Hobbes said, 'A man's labour also is a commodity exchangeable for benefit, as well as any other thing.'[3] Labour, or rather labour power, was external to the individual, and human freedom consisted in the opportunity of selling one's labour power to anyone who was prepared to buy it. Luther (1483–1546) had said, 'The soul will not be touched if the body is maltreated and the person subjected to another man's power.'[4] In this way the possessive individualism of the new social order divided the individual's private, inward life from his external, social attributes[5] and led to an unprecedented privatization or introjection of human experience.[6]

Possessive individualism has had a profound influence on systems of morality. Protestantism, for instance, tended to make moral virtue a matter of inner conscience and private spiritual struggle. Luther, as the young Marx put it, 'liberated man from exterior religiosity by making man's inner conscience religious. He emancipated the body from chains by enchaining the heart.'[7] Similarly the subjectivists and moral-sense theorists of the eighteenth century thought that the way to find out what was right and wrong was to look 'into your own breast'[8]; the romantics thought that the highest virtue was to be true to one's private, inner experience[9]; and the utilitarians tried to base morality on private feelings of pleasure and pain.[10] Thus the rise of capitalism was accompanied by an increasing preoccupation with individual subjectivity.[11]

Descartes's division of mental operations into actions and passions was part of this process. It was in effect an attempt to divide a person's thoughts into ones which expressed his real, inner nature and ones which did not, and to identify within the individual's mind a central core of true personality, a self, an inner self, or an ego, which could be distinguished from accidental accretions. Truly free human actions were ones which issued from this source.[12]

This introjected notion of the self remained only implicit in Descartes's writings. It was taken up and developed, however, by numerous empiricist writers. They required the notion because their habit of treating people's ideas as a sort of external world, or as objects which are acted on and perceived, made it necessary for them to think of a person not so much as a homunculus inside the body, but rather as a homunculus inside the mind (see above, pp.65-68). They thought of the mind as inside the body, and of the self as inside the mind.

Below the surface stream, shallow and light,
Of what we say we feel – below the stream,
As light, of what we think we feel – there flows
With noiseless current strong, obscure and deep,
The central stream of what we feel indeed.

Matthew Arnold[13]

The empiricist version of the introjected concept of the self played an important part in Locke's writings. Locke's position is slightly obscured, however, by his way of using the word 'mind' to refer to the inner self, which made him speak of ideas as though they were outside the mind. It would have been appropriate if he had taken over a phrase actually used by Descartes, and said that ideas are objects which pass before 'the mind's eye'.[14] Locke did in fact speak of a person's relationship to his ideas as though it involved a sort of seeing. He claimed that the mind could pay various degrees of attention to its ideas. Sometimes it would scrutinize them so intently that it 'shuts out all other thoughts', but

at other times it barely observes the train of ideas that succeed in the understanding, without directing and pursuing any of them, and at other times it lets them pass almost quite unregarded as faint shadows that make no impression ... At last, in the dark retirements of sound sleep, [the mind] loses sight perfectly of all ideas whatsoever.[15]

Locke thought that the mind learnt of its own operations in much the same way as it learnt about things in the 'external world':

When it turns its view inwards on itself, and observes its own actions about those ideas it has, [it] takes from thence other ideas, which are as capable to be the objects of its contemplation as any of those it received from foreign things.[16]

Thus Locke's empiricist version of the introjected notion of the self made it possible to think of one's own ideas as mysterious and alien things, and to picture oneself as their victim or their prisoner.

The empiricist notion of the self has had a strong influence on conceptions of mental health and illness. Before the eighteenth century, it was normal to think of madmen as people who were possessed by outside forces, probably divine or devilish. Mad behaviour was not an action of the madman, and therefore it was not something he could be held responsible for. Madness was not a personal flaw in the madman; and even conditions like vertigo were sometimes classified as madness. The new notion of the self changed this situation.

Locke's account of the self was taken over in the eighteenth century by the Cartesian materialists, who were amongst the first thinkers to treat psychology as a part of medical science. The Encyclopedist Denis Diderot (1715–84) gave an acute portrait of their theories in his novel *D'Alembert's Dream*. Diderot's main character, a doctor called Bordeu, was a convinced Cartesian materialist. He believed that all mental operations could be explained by a purely physical account of an 'organ of consciousness', or a 'self', which was situated in the middle of the nervous system, he said, like a spider in the middle of its web. Equipped with this model, Bordeu was in a good position to portray such psychological conditions as weary cynicism, detachment and depression. For example, he gave the following account of the causes of chronic depression:

> Almost everyone has at some time been in a deep depression. It only takes some chance occurrence to make this condition involuntary and habitual. Then, in spite of distractions and varied amusements, in spite of friendly advice, and his own personal efforts, the fibres (in the nerves) will persist in sending funereal vibrations to the centre of the web. The unlucky person struggles in vain; his world is covered in darkness and wherever he goes he is accompanied by a *cortège* of gloomy ideas; so in the end he does away with himself.[17]

Thus it seems that Bordeu tended to see human beings as helpless passengers in the ship of their body, rather than as pilots; as despairing castaways, gazing blankly at ideas floating down streams of consciousness. Bordeu's patients could not even call their ideas their own. So, it would seem, they could not be held responsible for their mental disorders.

Nevertheless, Bordeu did think that his patients were somehow responsible for their condition. His theory of sanity was that when

> the centre of the bundle (of nerves) gives orders and all the other parts obey (then) the creature is master of itself, compos mentis.[18]

Madness was therefore loss of control, and there was only one way to treat it:

> I know of only one remedy, and it is perfectly safe, though rather difficult to administer. It can only work if the centre of the sensitive

web, the self [*le soi*] can be induced by some violent motive to recover its authority.[19]

Bordeu reported that he had had great success when he applied this remedy to a woman who suffered from frequent attacks of the vapours.

The rebellion always began in her fibres [*filets*] and she could always feel it coming on. She would stand up, run about, and busy herself with the most vigorous forms of physical exercise; she would climb up and down stairs, saw wood, and shovel earth. Then the organ of her will, at the centre of the bundle, would become rigid as she said to herself: 'Victory, or death!'[20]

Thus, contrary to what one might expect, Bordeu's view of madness concentrated responsibility for being mad on the madman: he ought simply to pull himself together.

Michel Foucault has tried to explain the emergence in the eighteenth century of the idea that madmen are responsible for their madness, by reference to the fact that the cause of madness came to be located inside the madman rather than outside him. Specifically, madness was coming to be thought of as the result of disorders in the individual's brain or nervous system. Explanations of 'nervous diseases' were couched in terms of Descartes's theory that the behaviour of the nervous system could be explained in terms of the tension of fibres and the pressure of animal spirits in the nerves and the brain. This theory supplied psychology with an array of new imagery – pressure, suppression, blockage, tension, release and so on[21] – and also suggested a general hypothesis about the causes of liability to mental illness.

General alertness or sensitivity was naturally thought of as a result of having delicate nervous machinery, and in particular of having 'highly strung' nerve-fibres, which would vibrate in sympathy with the minutest stimulus. As Bordeu explains, this means that a sensitive person is always in danger of getting into a state where 'every fibre in his nervous system is agitated ... the centre of the bundle does not know what is going to become of it'.[22] In this way the Cartesian materialists tried to locate the roots of madness in the individual's mental constitution. As Foucault puts it, they held that 'the mind becomes blind through very excess of sensibility'.[23]

Foucault maintains that these views about the causes of madness led directly to the idea that the madman is responsible for his disorder, and hence brought about a 'moralization of madness'. But this suggestion is too simple, because it does not explain the characteristic ambivalence of the new attitudes to madness. Bordeu's account, for example, contains numerous suggestions that madness is simply something that happens to people, and that it is in no way an action expressing their moral character. Similarly, when Voltaire said that madness was a physical illness comparable to gout, he was doing the opposite of moralizing madness.[24] The common source of these opposed tendencies is the new introjected notion of the self. This, by suggesting that people might be strangers to some of the operations of their minds, identified them even more strongly with others. If someone was estranged from what went on before his mind's eye, he would for that reason be more intimately identified with what went on behind it. The new notion of the self made it possible either to moralize madness, or to remove it altogether from morality. The new concept of madness, therefore, was more like the old one than Foucault suggests. It was perfectly capable of representing mad behaviour as a passion of the madman due to alien forces. The distinctive thing about the new attitudes to madness was that, owing to the rise of a new concept of the self, it enabled people to treat items in their own mental life as outside forces.

The empiricist version of the introjected notion of the self makes a person's true nature systematically elusive. It enables one to say of any personal attribute, such as having a poor memory, or being a good singer, or being clever, or cruel, or hasty, that it does not belong to its owner's real self, but to something outside it, which he is not responsible for, or which he cannot help. The self as conceived by empiricism recedes from every concrete description with which one tries to capture it. The centre of the individual psyche becomes impossible to identify. Not all notions of the inner self have this feature, however. In particular, the notion implicit in Descartes's later writings was quite different. Descartes thought that the self could be identified in terms of an ideal of good sense and rationality shared by all human beings (see below, pp.143-144).

Descartes's view of the mind tends to be mentioned today only as an example of the extremely facile nature of old-fashioned ideas about subjectivity. People assert that Descartes's view of the mind is incompatible with the sorts of phenomena which Freud explained in terms of repression and the unconscious, and that whereas Descartes thought it was impossible for a person to be unaware of the contents of his mind, Freud's discoveries have proved him wrong.

There is at least one way in which this criticism of Descartes is undoubtedly correct, for Descartes asserted categorically that 'the mind is better known than the body'.[25] He explained his motive for making this assertion when he dedicated the *Meditations* to the theology faculty at the Sorbonne. His Dedication referred to the fact that the eighth session of the Lateran Council had condemned the opinion that the nature and existence of the soul cannot be known by reason, and had appealed to Christian philosophers to 'make known the truth'.[26] Descartes claimed that the *Meditations* satisfied this request, because it proved that, beside knowledge of God, knowledge of the soul was 'the most certain and evident of all the things that can be known by the human mind'.[27] This claim was based on his late theory of ideas, according to which knowledge always involves ideas and therefore the mind. Descartes thought that this proved that everyone knows more about his mind than about anything else:

One knows more attributes of one's mind than of anything else, because however many one knows in other things, one can count as many in the mind since it knows them; and for this reason its nature is better known than other things.[28] There is nothing which enables us to obtain knowledge of things other than the mind, which does not with much more certainty give us knowledge of our mind.[29]

The feebleness of Descartes's argument is transparently obvious. It simply does not follow from his view that knowledge always involves having ideas, that it involves knowing about them. One might well be unable to give an accurate account of one's ideas. So perhaps Descartes's belief that the mind is 'more easily known than the body' can be regarded as no more than a spurious offshoot of his late philosophy.

Descartes's belief that the mind is better known than the body was also connected with his attempt to define the mind as the field of supremely certain knowledge (see above, pp.95-96). Although Descartes never offered any reasons to justify his use of this definition, he relied on it extensively and it is undoubtedly central to his late philosophy. It might seem obvious that no account of the mind which is based on such a definition could accommodate descriptions of processes like repression, displacement, or unconscious motivation and self deception, in which the state of one's own mind is opaque, mysterious or deceptive.

But such arguments against Descartes are far too simple; and they misrepresent not only his view of the mind but also Freud's. For Descartes's definition of the mind in terms of certain knowledge, properly understood, is essentially directed against the empiricist attempt to treat a person's knowledge of his own states of mind on the model normally applied to a person's knowledge of independent objects in the 'external world', rather than against the possibility of unconscious thoughts. Descartes's definition of the mind implied that thinking about one's present state of mind is quite different from thinking about other things, and that it does not run the same risk of going wrong, simply because it is not thinking about independent objects.

In the Third Meditation, Descartes analysed mental acts into a component contributed by the intellect and a component contributed by the will (see above, pp.92-93). The function of the intellectual component was to represent objects outside the mind, and the function of the willing component was to express an attitude to what was represented by the intellect. If the attitude was assertion or denial, one was making a judgement, which might or might not correspond to independent objective facts; if the attitude was aversion or attraction, one was simply having a volition.

The contribution of the will to judgements was very different from the contribution of the intellect. For this reason, Descartes was reluctant to call the items contributed by the will ideas. He did not hesitate to say that there were ideas in the intellect, representing things like God or a piece of beeswax. These ideas, he said, were 'like pictures of things: it is to these alone that the word "idea" is strictly appropriate'.[30] Ideas in the will, however, were not like pictures: they did not depict or represent things. An empiricist, however, would deny this. He would say that such ideas represent the actions of the will. Descartes's reply would be that, far from representing the actions of the will, they actually constitute them. When you have the idea of assertion, he would say, you are not observing a judgement taking place in your mind, but simply making a judgement. Descartes even went so far as to say that there is no distinction between thinking you are in a certain mental state, and actually being in that state. 'Willing something is *eo ipso* perceiving that we will it.'[31] 'We could not will anything without knowing that we willed it, nor know it except by means of an idea; but I do not say that this idea is anything different from the action.'[32] With these statements, Descartes went further than he was really entitled to. But an important and valid insight underlies them: that your present state of mind – unlike, say, God or the piece of beeswax – is not independent of your thoughts about it.

It is obvious that Descartes was wrong to suggest that people are conscious of all their mental states; but he may still have been right in his view of the difference between thinking about one's present state of mind and thinking about other things. However, there are phenomena which can seem to count against Descartes's contention. If I used to think I was in love with someone, but now realize that I was not in love, then it seems clear that I used to be mistaken about my state of mind; and such mistakes would be impossible if one's mental states could not have a character different from that which one supposes them to have. It might be suggested that the only possible way of explaining this is to adopt an empiricist view of the mind, and to think of oneself as a beleaguered homunculus in the alien territory of one's mind.[33] But in fact such phenomena can be explained without recourse to empiricism.

On a non-empiricist account, making a mistake about, say, whether one is in love, is not a matter of making a conjecture which turns out to be false about some objects quite independent of one's thoughts. Instead, mistakes about the character of one's mental states can be explained as mistakes about the significance of one's thoughts, due to ignorance of their systematic interrelationships. To discover that one was mistaken in thinking one was in love is to discover that one's belief that one was in love does not fit in with others of one's thoughts.

Part of the justification for such a non-empiricist approach is that it is sensitive to the ways in which a person's mistakes about his present state of mind, unlike other mistakes, cannot be isolated or unmotivated. Unlike the empiricist approach, it does not assimilate mistaking say, jealousy for love, to things like mistaking an aeroplane flying in the sky for a bird.

We must get clear about how the metaphor of revealing (inside and outside) is actually applied by us; otherwise we shall be tempted to look for an inside behind *that which in our metaphor is the inside.*

Wittgenstein[34]

The main reason for rejecting the empiricist approach to the problems of knowing one's own state of mind is that it provides no more than a mirage of a solution. It suggests that when you are thinking about your present state of mind, you

133

are thinking about independent objects. But it cannot possibly supply any characterization of these allegedly independent objects, which does not amount simply to a description of the thoughts of the person who is supposed to be experiencing them or thinking about them.[35] Descartes's account of the mind is facile in that it fails to recognize the difficulties of providing clear and lucid descriptions of thoughts, both one's own and other people's; but this does not mean that its weakness can be summed up as a failure to acknowledge the existence of the unconscious.

Empiricist theories of the mind, such as Locke's theory, contain a concept which might be called a concept of the unconscious. This is the concept of those ideas or mental states which, for some reason, the mind's eye cannot or will not look at. Freud himself sometimes wrote as though his own concept of the unconscious were the same as this empiricist concept. In 1915 he wrote: 'In psychoanalysis, there is no choice for us but to assert that mental processes are in themselves unconscious, and to liken the perception of them by means of consciousness to the perception of the external world by means of sense organs.'[36] A similar interpretation of the psychoanalytic theory of the unconscious is presupposed by people who call Freud the 'discoverer of the unconscious' and treat him as a sort of Captain Cook of the mind. But such interpretations are of very little value in explaining what it was that Freud discovered. It is an interpretation which would fit Locke's theory better than Freud's. If it is applied to Freud, it makes a complete mystery of the history of Western ideas about consciousness; for, long before Freud, writers like Spinoza, Leibniz, Hegel and Marx produced accounts of latent or hidden levels of human consciousness. And even though Descartes failed to appreciate the complexities which later theories revealed, he did help produce the raw materials out of which they were made.

[14]

The Idea of God

Descartes arrived at his late theory of the mind by exploring the implications of idealism, which, in the rather artificial sense I am giving to the word, is the view that nothing exists except thinking or mind. Then he tried to use his theory of mind to disprove idealism. His argument was that the nature of the ideas or thoughts which make up the mind is such that they could not possibly be the only things that existed.

Descartes's argument involved a notion of the 'objective reality' of ideas. This notion, which was derived from the scholastics,[1] is very easy for modern readers to misunderstand, because the connotations which the word 'objective' now has make it natural to assume that when Descartes spoke of the 'objective reality' of ideas he was referring to something in what would now be called the 'objective world' as opposed to the world of thought. But in fact, Descartes evidently thought that even if idealism were true, and there was no such thing as an 'objective world' in the modern sense, ideas would still have objective reality. Several paraphrases of 'objective' have been proposed in order to avoid this difficulty. It has even been suggested that Descartes's meaning is captured by the word 'subjective'. However, something very like what Descartes meant is still conveyed when the word is used in phrases like 'aims and objectives'. The closest modern equivalents of Descartes's 'objective reality' are perhaps 'intention' (or 'intension'), 'meaning' and 'sense'. Objective reality, as Descartes conceived it, was the property of ideas which made 'some (ideas) represent one thing, others another'.[2]

The objective reality of an idea was specified by a description of what it stood for. Descartes thought that in general it was possible to specify the objective reality of an idea while leaving it an open question whether anything in reality corresponds to it. For instance, the objective reality of a winged horse or of a daffodil can be specified by describing what would make it true that a winged horse exists or that a daffodil exists; and this objective reality would exist whether or not there was such a thing as a winged horse or a daffodil. Descartes's attempt to doubt as much as possible can be described as an attempt to isolate the objective reality of ideas by denying that anything corresponds to them; and his argument against idealism was that this attempt could not succeed with every idea. According to Descartes, one could not grasp the objective reality of the idea of God without realizing that God exists, so if one had the idea of God, one would have (if only implicitly) sure knowledge that he exists. Thus, Descartes concluded, the idea of God is the one case where it is valid to argue from one's knowledge of one's ideas to the existence of something outside them.

One of Descartes's versions of this argument is normally called the causal argument. It is based on the 'causal principle', which states that a cause must have 'at least as much reality as its effect'.[3] Descartes had applied this principle to matter and motion, and he now proposed to apply it to ideas, saying that the objective reality of every idea must have a cause with 'as much reality as its effect'.[4] Descartes said that the objective reality of many ideas, such as ideas of people, animals or angels, might be caused by the objective reality of others: 'I can easily conceive of these as composed of the ideas I have of myself, of physical things, and of God – even if, apart from me, there might be no men, animals, or angels in the world.'[5] But this process could not go on for ever: 'Although it may be possible for one idea to give birth to another, this process cannot go on to infinity, but must instead arrive at a first idea.'[6] Descartes then applied his causal principle to this 'first idea' and asked what the cause of its own objective reality could be. He was sure it could not lie in the realm of ideas.[7] But, he thought, the only thing outside the realm of ideas which was sufficiently powerful to be its cause must be what the 'first idea' represents;

and this, according to Descartes, was God. Thus Descartes thought that the existence of something other than thinking or the mind – namely, God – could be proved on the basis of an assumption which idealists were bound to concede. 'From the fact that I exist and have in me an idea of a supremely perfect being, that is of God, it can be demonstrated conclusively that God exists.'[8]

It is not difficult to find fault with Descartes's 'conclusive demonstration'. Descartes thought that the causal principle was 'manifest by the natural light'; he offered no argument for it apart from the rhetorical question 'Where can the effect get its reality from, if not from its cause?'[9] But this question is based on a weird and implausible view of what reality is: it makes reality sound like a fluid which can be transferred from one thing to another, like water being poured into a cup. And even if this conception of reality were acceptable, Descartes would have no justification for applying it to ideas, so as to arrive at the question 'Where does the objective reality of ideas come from?' In doing so he was assuming that objective reality is a sort of reality, which is rather like assuming that imaginary animals are a sort of animal. Descartes's argument seems similar to the following: since some people have had heart-attacks when they imagined they saw a ghost, and since heart-attacks are real, then there must be real ghosts to cause them.

In the Fifth Meditation Descartes produced a version of his argument for the existence of God which avoided making use of the causal principle. This version is normally called the ontological argument. It is very similar to the causal argument; and since Descartes seems to have thought that there was only one proof of the existence of God,[10] it is best regarded as simply a restatement, or an explanation, of the causal argument.[11] The ontological argument starts from the claim that the unique thing about the idea of God is that it is the idea of something which necessarily exists, or which could not conceivably not exist, or 'to whose essence alone existence belongs'.[12] The implications of this, according to Descartes, were as follows:

'Existence can no more be separated from the essence of God than the fact that its three angles are equal to two right angles can be separated from the essence of a triangle, or than the idea of a mountain can be separated from the idea of a valley.'[13] According to this definition of God, it follows immediately from our having the idea of God that he exists. But the conclusion follows so easily that one cannot help suspecting Descartes of a sleight of hand.

Descartes's basic argument for the existence of God has two stages. The object of the first is to establish that we have the idea of God as something which could not conceivably not exist; and the object of the second is to prove that it follows that God does exist. This second stage has raised a flurry of objections, mostly based on the idea that one cannot prove anything as to what exists in the real world simply on the basis of one's ideas. As Kant put it, the 'famous ontological argument of Descartes' is 'merely so much labour and effort lost; we can no more extend our stock of (theoretical) insight by mere ideas, than a merchant can better his position by adding a few noughts to his cash account'.[14] But this sort of criticism is unconvincing, for two reasons. First, the statement that knowledge cannot be extended by 'mere ideas' needs a lot of qualification if it is to be accepted, since as it stands there are many exceptions to it. For example, anyone who thinks about the subject for a moment will realize, perhaps for the first time, that if he traces back his ancestry through the past, then, as long as neither he nor any of his ancestors has parents who are blood relations, each time he goes one generation further back, he will find that the number of his ancestors doubles. Thus it seems to be possible after all to acquire knowledge by reflection on 'mere ideas'. Secondly, Descartes himself might well have agreed with the general principle that it is impossible to learn about reality by simply reflecting on ideas; his contention was that the idea of God was the unique exception. This, indeed, provided him with his definition of God. If it is permissible to define something as that which exists if it can be conceived, and

if one can conceive of such a thing, then it inescapably follows
that it exists.[15]

The only way to fault Descartes's argument is to return to
the first stage of it and to investigate what, if anything, the
idea of God can mean in the context of the argument. It might
be argued that Descartes's idea of God does not make sense, and
cannot mean anything, because in effect it identifies God with
the idea of God[16]; and if a thing were identical with the idea of
it, it would also be identical with the idea of the idea of it, and
so on *ad infinitum*. But the first stage of the basic argument, as
it is presented in the Third Meditation, suggests another interpretation of Descartes's idea of God. Descartes said God was
'an archetype, so to speak, which actually contains all the
reality which is contained only objectively in ideas'.[17] Thus
Descartes identified God with what must exist if ideas are to be
capable of representing things, or of having objective reality.
It seems to follow that Descartes's God is defined simply as that
which is presupposed by the meaningfulness of our ideas. If
this is so, then in spite of its use of the word 'God', Descartes's
argument is not really a religious argument at all – though
Descartes obviously thought that it was. It is more like the
'transcendental' arguments against idealism of later philosophers. If it proves anything, it is only that the ability to think

---

*Couldn't I say: If I had to add the world to my language it would have
to be one sign for the whole of language, which sign could therefore be
left out?*
Idealism leads to realism if it is strictly thought out.

Wittgenstein[18]

---

involves the ability to use the concept of an 'objective world',
or of reality outside thought; and that this would be impossible
if there were not an objective world. Although this may be a
good way of attacking idealism, it has no tendency to prove
the existence of God.

The hidden truth about Descartes's arguments for the
existence of God is that they are an elucidation of his theory of
ideas rather than a contribution to theology. Descartes said:

'By the word "God" I mean a substance that is infinite, (eternal, immutable,) all knowing and all powerful.'[19] And on several occasions he used the phrase *'Deus aut Natura'* – God or nature.[20] Thus Descartes's God had very little in common with the God of traditional Christianity; it was not the sort of God who could be good or bad, jealous or forgiving, or who could respond to prayers and intervene in human affairs. Though Descartes probably never realized it, his God could not provide the consolations of religion. It is not surprising that Pascal wrote: 'I cannot forgive Descartes. In all his philosophy he would have been quite willing to dispense with God.'[21]

[15]

Knowledge and Humanism

Descartes's early philosophy was sceptical in the sense that it acquiesced in the opinion that human beings might be unable to know the true nature of things, and that human thought might be inescapably a system of illusions. For this reason, Descartes's early work, the *Rules for the Direction of the Mind*, contains attempts to draw a distinction between the real natures of things and the way they appear to human beings, and suggests that there may be an unbridgeable gap between the two. Descartes wrote: 'Individual things are to be seen in a different way from the point of view of our knowledge (*cognitionem*) than if we were to speak of them as they really are.' He went on to suggest that even his own quantitative, reductionist approach to science was concerned with the appearances of things rather than with their true nature:

> Since our present concern is with things insofar as we understand them [*quantum ab intellectu percipiuntur*] we can call things simple when we have such a lucid and distinct knowledge of them [*cognitio ... perspicua ... & distincta*] that they cannot be divided into others more distinctly known by the mind. Such are shape, extension, movement, etc. We regard all others as composed out of these.[1]

Thus the young Descartes seems to have thought that the justification of his ideal of scientific explanation depended on facts about the human mind and not on facts about the natural world.

In his later work, Descartes tried to prove that human beings were able to discover the true nature of things, and not just the appearances which they presented 'from the point of view of our knowledge'.[2] On a superficial reading, however, Descartes's attempts to prove this conclusion were hopelessly inadequate.

His main argument seems to have been that God could not have been so deceitful as to withhold from human beings the ability to know the true natures of things; that God could not have endowed human beings with inaccurate ideas, at least not without at the same time equipping them with the ability to correct them. This argument, which is known as the argument from God's benevolence, has often been criticized for being circular, since Descartes could not have claimed to have proved the existence of God from the idea of God without at least presupposing that his idea of God was accurate (see below, pp. 146-148).[3] Apart from this difficulty, the argument can be rejected on the grounds that God might not after all give human beings the ability to know the true natures of things. It is doubtful whether it makes sense to ascribe any actions at all to a being as abstract as the God whose existence Descartes thought he had proved; and in any case this God might not act benevolently. And, even if he did act benevolently, he might not equip human beings with a capacity for knowledge of the true natures of things. His benevolence might make him prefer a world which contained two types of thinking beings, some with a capacity for knowledge and others without it; and human beings might be creatures of the second type.[4]

The argument from God's benevolence cannot achieve its purpose, but it was only part of Descartes's response to scepticism. It was interwoven with two other strands, which in spite of having a somewhat archaic appearance are of continuing importance. These two strands are known as the theory of innate ideas and the theory of the creation of eternal truths.

The theory of innate ideas was present in Descartes's earliest writings, in the form of the view that the human mind naturally contains 'seeds' which, if properly cultivated, grow into knowledge.[5] (Descartes sometimes expressed the same idea by saying that human inquiry should be guided by a 'natural light'.) In Descartes's late philosophy, this view developed into the theory that God equipped human beings with innate ideas, and thereby gave them the capacity to know the natures of things. It is not surprising that Descartes's examples of innate ideas – God, the soul,[6] continuous quantity, extension in length, breadth and depth, size, shape and movement[7] – correspond to his examples of clear and distinct ideas,[8] since these too were regarded as the materials of which all knowledge is composed. Nor is it surprising that the notion of innate ideas has the same vagueness as the notion of clear and distinct ideas (see above, p.88). Descartes thought that many or even all ideas were composed of elements which in themselves were clear and distinct; and similarly, since 'they all appear to proceed from me in the same way',[9] Descartes thought that all ideas might be regarded as innate.[10] From this point of view, having ideas was the same as having innate ideas, and the same as having a capacity to think, or a mind. Descartes claimed: 'I have never written, nor been of the opinion, that the mind needs innate ideas in the sense of something distinct from the faculty of thinking.'[11] It might have been better if Descartes had used the word 'natural' instead of 'innate', because it was not essential to his argument against scepticism to say that people had a mind from the moment they were born, rather than that they only acquired it after they had been alive for some time. However, since his belief that a person's essence is thinking implied that a person could not exist without thinking, and since he also believed with the orthodox that a person comes into being at or before birth, he had to say that people were born with a mind, and hence with ideas.[12]

Descartes's theory of innate or natural ideas was, amongst other things, an explanation of his version of the introjected notion of the self. The inner self, for Descartes, was constituted by innate ideas. A person was active when he was giving expression to his natural capacity for thought or his innate ideas, and thus having only ideas which were clear and distinct; and he was passive when his thinking was distorted by outside forces, such as those which give rise to the confused ideas which are based on unreflective sensory experience. This account differs importantly from the empiricist accounts developed by certain later thinkers (see above, pp. 129-130) because it does not make the inner self systematically elusive and quite incapable of being defined.

Descartes linked his theory of innate ideas with another theory, according to which God had contrived things in such a way that clear and distinct ideas must correspond to their true nature: .

> I have noticed certain laws, *which God has so established in nature*, and of which he has established such notions in our souls, that having reflected on them sufficiently it is impossible for us to doubt that they are obeyed with exactness in everything which exists or which happens in the world.[13]

This theory, the theory of the creation of eternal truths, implied that 'eternal truths' were true only because God chose to make them so. Most theologians found this theory highly unorthodox. And it might seem that the theory was not only unorthodox but also nonsensical. Descartes gave arithmetical truths as examples of 'eternal truths' created by God, and he apparently thought that God might have decided to create an eternal truth corresponding to '$2 + 2 = 5$' instead of '$2 + 2 = 4$'. But this does not really make sense: if the result of adding a number to itself was something other than four, the number in question could not possibly be two, regardless of what God might have decided. God could only have made the sentence '$2 + 2 = 5$' express a truth by changing the meaning of at least one of the symbols in it, for instance by making '5' represent the number four. But obviously Descartes's theory of the creation of eternal truths was meant to say something more important than this.

In order to understand the point of Descartes's theory of 'eternal truths' it is necessary to remember that he did not have a sophisticated classification of truths at his disposal. He knew nothing of the relatively precise modern concepts of necessary, *a priori*, analytic, logical, formal or mathematical truths, and of natural laws. He put all these types of truths in the same category, and he thought of his theory as applying to all of them. Thus he sometimes spoke of the creation of 'what you call "eternal truths"',[14] and sometimes of the creation of essences[15] or laws of nature.[16]

The orthodox, Platonistic, view of eternal truths was that whereas everything that exists in time, including the minds of men, had been created by God, the eternal truths or essences of things had not.[17] This suggested that knowledge of eternal truths or essences was quite separate from knowledge of what actually exists,[18] and it also tended to lead to pessimism about man's knowledge of the eternal truths. If they lay beyond creation, it seemed likely that they were beyond the grasp of the human mind.

They [the thinkers before Descartes] ... laid it down as an axiom that judgements of God far surpass human understanding. This doctrine might have concealed the truth from the human race for all eternity, if mathematics, which is concerned not with final causes but with the essences and properties of figures, had not provided them with another standard of truth.

Spinoza[19]

Descartes's theory of the creation of eternal truths was designed to deprive scepticism of the foothold provided by the Platonistic theory of the eternal truths. If essences were part of the created world, then they were on the same level as other things, and equally within the reach of human knowledge. Thus, as one writer puts it, the important thing about Descartes's theory is that it 'humanizes essences'[20]; it makes way for the humanistic view that there are no mysteries which it is impossible for human beings to understand.

The essences of things, according to Descartes, were not mysterious. On the contrary, an inquiry into essences was nothing but an inquiry into the clear and distinct ideas which were the natural or innate endowment of the human mind. The limits of what was possible in nature were simply the limits of what human beings could conceive; they could be discovered by conceivability tests or the method of doubt.[21] Thus Descartes came to give up his early opinion that the order of nature might not correspond to the order of human knowledge. In his late philosophy, it was impossible to distinguish between the two; it was valid to argue 'from knowledge to reality'[22]; and all things were 'in fact, and in truth, as they present themselves to our mind (*perceptionem*)'.[23]

The humanistic theory of knowledge is the main thesis of

I remember when I was a young Oxford Scholar, that he could not endure to heare of the New [*Cartesian*] Philosophy: *For, sayd he, if a new Philosophy is brought in, a new Divinity will shortly follow; and he was right.*

John Aubrey[24]

Descartes's late philosophy. It dismisses scepticism by saying that the natures or essences of things can be discovered simply by investigating what it is possible for human beings to think; and that the only standards which can be applied to human thought are human standards. But the theory seems vulnerable to the charge of circularity, which was mentioned in connection with the argument from God's benevolence (see above, p.142). For while the humanistic theory of knowledge is a conclusion of Descartes's late philosophy, it also functions as a premiss in his main arguments, in particular his arguments for his concept of the soul and for the existence of God. These arguments presuppose that human beings can obtain knowledge of the essences of things simply by reflecting on what it is possible for them to conceive. In other words, they presuppose the validity of conceivability tests or the method of doubt.

When Descartes tried to establish his concept of the soul (see above, p. 76), he began with a premiss – which I criticized in Chapter Eleven – about conceivability: the soul, he said, might conceivably exist even if nothing but thinking existed; and he concluded that the essence of the soul was thinking. But he anticipated an objection to a basic assumption of his argument. 'The . . . objection is that it does not follow from the fact that the human mind reflecting on itself does not perceive itself to be anything other than a thing that thinks, that its nature or essence consists only in its being a thing that thinks.'[25] This objection is an application of the general sceptical view that while techniques like the method of doubt, or conceivability tests, may reveal how things appear to the human mind, they cannot prove anything about how things are in themselves. Descartes said he could only answer the objection when he had proved the existence of a God who had equipped human beings with clear and distinct ideas which reflected the true essences of things,[26] and hence proved the validity of conceivability tests.

However, this suggestion seems to carry Descartes round the same circle all over again. His attempt to prove the existence of God clearly rests on the very assumption which he wants to defend. It presupposes that the fact that it is impossible for human beings to conceive of God as not existing proves that existence is part of God's essence. In the Fifth Meditation, Descartes anticipated an objection on precisely these lines: 'Although I conceive of God as (necessarily) existing, it might seem that it does not follow that he exists, for my thinking cannot impose necessity on things.'[27] Clearly this objection is just another application of the general sceptical view that facts about what human beings can conceive do not reveal how things really are, but only how they appear to the human mind. And while he was trying to prove the existence of God, Descartes could not try to ward off the objection by saying that it would be answered when God's existence had been proved. If the objection was valid, then his argument for the existence of God could not possibly succeed. So Descartes simply reiterated his humanistic faith in human thought: 'From the fact that I cannot think of God without existence it follows that existence is inseparable from him.'[28] It seems therefore that Descartes's humanism about knowledge was completely circular.

It is perhaps surprising that Descartes was unperturbed by the rather obvious circularity of his attempts to justify his view of human knowledge. It could be argued that in fact his argument is not really circular, because it is an attempt to prove a specific conclusion about the correctness of certain ideas, namely the basic ideas of his physics, on the basis of a general humanistic assumption that clear and distinct ideas correspond to the essences of things. Descartes's statement that he did not prove his laws of nature in *The World*, though he would do so in another place,[29] and his claim that the *Meditations* contained the foundations of his physics[30] support this interpretation.

But Descartes's main reason for not being perturbed by the apparent circularity of his arguments for his humanistic theory of knowledge is that the nature of his humanism is such that no other sorts of argument could possibly be produced for it. All he could sensibly do was try to establish the negative claims that it is impossible for human beings to have any reason for doubting that their ideas reflect the nature of things.[31] If he had tried to justify his humanistic theory of knowledge by reference to something outside human experience, he would have been undermining his own case, which was that there are no such external standards.

Descartes's theory of the creation of eternal truths was an integral part of his late philosophy; but he hardly mentioned it in his published writings.[32] He had once intended to explain the theory in *The World*, but he decided to sound out the opinion of theologians before doing so. He soon found that they objected to his theory. Perhaps they realized that by saying that everyone could obtain knowledge of the essences of things simply by using their natural mental powers, Descartes, like Luther before him, was undermining the theologian's position as professional guardian of mysteries inaccessible to ordinary people.[33] Another reason which the theologians had for objecting to the theory of the creation of eternal truths was that it completely dehumanized God. Paradoxically, this is precisely the aspect of his theory which Descartes thought theologians ought to welcome. He thought that by saying that 'the truths of mathematics, which you call eternal, have been established by God and depend on him entirely, just as much as the rest of his creatures', he was doing a service to Christianity, by distinguishing it sharply from paganism. 'To say that these truths are independent of him amounts to treating God as a Jupiter or a Saturn, and to subjecting him to the Styx and the Fates.'[34] However, in recommending a concept of God so very far removed from those of paganism, Descartes was making it impossible to attach any sense at all to the idea of God performing actions based on rational choices. God's choice of eternal truths or laws of nature would not be governed by any reasons for choosing one rather than another, because however he chose he would be bound to be right. There would be no standard of rightness apart from what he chose. This meant that God's choices were arbitrary and blind.[35] They were exercises of 'liberty of indifference' as opposed to 'liberty of spontaneity'; and Descartes himself had said that liberty of indifference was the lowest form of liberty (see above, p.120). Descartes was perfectly aware of these implications of his theory.[36] 'Supreme indifference in God,' he said, 'is the supreme proof of his omnipotence.'[37] He had brought knowledge of essences down to the level of human thought; but at

---

Philosophy first builds itself up within the religious form of consciousness, and in so doing on the one hand destroys religion as such, while on the other hand, in its positive content, it still moves only within the religious sphere.

Karl Marx[38]

---

the same time had raised God beyond its reach. Knowledge of the alternatives open to God would require ideas which the human mind was incapable of forming. 'It is pointless to ask how God could have brought it about from all eternity that two times four should not have been eight, etc., for I admit that this is something we cannot understand.'[39] As Descartes saw it, this enabled him to acknowledge the existence of a special type of knowledge, acquired by revelation, and quite independent of the scientific knowledge which could be acquired on the basis of clear and distinct ideas. He might have been more consistent, however, if he had said that knowledge of God's activities was impossible, and that talk of God was therefore completely pointless. But he declared that he did not want to 'get involved in theology', and thus he never faced up to the fact that his humanization of essences, and his dehumanization of God, endangered not only traditional theology but also all belief in God.

Descartes's writings are strewn with the remains of older systems of philosophy. He never stated his humanism about knowledge in a straightforward and direct way, but relied on the dubious paraphernalia of things like the argument from God's benevolence and the theory of the creation of eternal truths. But in the midst of all this Descartes was constructing a profoundly original conception of human nature. His originality was not that he asserted opinions which previous thinkers had considered and then rejected, but that he created an outlook which had formerly been inconceivable. Human nature was no longer to be thought of as confined by a divine plan, backed up by the authority of established religion. The assessment of human activities had to be grounded in human life. If Descartes was a chaotic thinker, the chaos was a product of creative struggle.

[16]

Descartes and History

In the seventeenth century, Descartes was widely thought of as the creator of the new scientific outlook, or of the 'new philosophy'. By the end of the century 'Cartesianism' was nearly synonymous with 'science'.[1] All over Europe, Descartes's work had been taken over by popularizers and teachers. In 1665, for example, Pierre-Sylvain Régis, a disciple of Descartes, gave a series of public lectures on Cartesian physics in Toulouse, and the lectures achieved a level of popularity normally reserved for great preachers. The educated townspeople were enthralled; intellectuals, magistrates, ecclesiastics and 'even ladies' crowded in to hear.[2]

But Cartesianism was not popular everywhere. In spite of his sincere attempts to prove that his opinions were orthodox, Descartes was seen by many as a subversive and atheistic thinker. His humanism about knowledge threatened the intellectual authority of the Church, and his mechanistic physics endangered the anthropocentric Christian world picture. For this reason Pascal saw it as his duty 'to write against those who made too profound a study of science: Descartes'.[3] This attitude was adopted with particular fervour in England, where Descartes's belief that the physical world could be understood without reference to final causes, and in particular without reference to divine purpose, was widely ridiculed. Henry More, for example, exclaimed: 'As if this material world, provided merely that one supposed as much motion communicated to matter as indeed one finds in it, could have engendered itself! Yet such is the Cartesian hypothesis!'[4] Newton expressed the same sort of attitude, saying that the study of God 'does certainly belong to Natural Philosophy', and that God is only known 'by his most wise and excellent contrivances of things, and final causes . . . A God without dominion, providence, and final causes, is nothing but Fate and Nature.'[5]

Various reactionary authorities felt so threatened by the alleged godlessness of Cartesianism that they took measures to suppress it. As early as 1643, the magistrates of Utrecht ordered the destruction of Descartes's works. In 1663, Descartes's works were put on the Index, because they were thought to be contrary to the principles of the Catholic religion, and in 1671, in spite of the fashion for Cartesianism amongst the ladies of the French court, Louis XIV issued an edict forbidding the teaching of Cartesian physics.[6] In the two European countries which had experienced bourgeois revolutions, however – the Netherlands and England – Cartesianism spread freely. Even opponents of Cartesianism had to admit that the influence of Descartes was transforming both philosophy and science. The following passage was written by a French Jesuit in 1691:

Judging by the medical and philosophical books reaching us from England, Holland, and Germany, Cartesianism has made great strides in these quarters. Philosophy courses based on the scholastic method are hardly printed any more, and nearly all the works of this kind which come out of France these days are treatises on physics based on the principles of the new philosophy. People no longer talk about Thomists, Scotists, and nominalists, except in the schools; or at least people no longer distinguish between them; they put them all in the same category and on the same side, calling it ancient philosophy; to this they oppose the philosophy of Descartes, or the new philosophy.[7]

Descartes's influence could be seen even in fields about which he had written nothing. For example, the Preface to Sir Dudley North's *Discourses upon Trade* (1691) says that the attempt to explain economic facts in terms of first principles, rather than in terms of superstitions about gold and trade, was due to the influence of Descartes's method:

I find Trade here treated at another rate, than usually hath been; I mean philosophically . . . He [Sir Dudley North] reduceth things to their Extreams, wherein all discriminations are most gross and sensible, and then shews them; and not in the state of ordinary concerns, whereof the terms are scarce distinguishable. This Method of Reasoning hath been introduc'd with the new Philosophy, the Old dealt in Abstracts more than Truths; and was employed about forming Hypotheses, to fit abundance of precarious and insensible Principles . . . ; whereby they made sure of nothing: but upon the appearance of *Descartes's* excellent dissertation *de Methodo*, so much approved and accepted in our Ages, all those Chymera's soon dissolved and vanisht.[8]

Such views of Descartes's significance led to a reinterpretation of the whole history of philosophy. A notion of 'the Dark Ages' or 'the Middle Ages' had come into being in the Renaissance, and had been used to dismiss everything that happened between the decline of ancient civilization and the Renaissance; and in the seventeenth and eighteenth centuries it was extended to cover everything that happened between the decline of ancient civilization and the rise of Cartesianism. The *philosophes* of the eighteenth century saw Descartes as the great pioneer of the enlightenment. Their view was summed up in a prize-winning oration on Descartes, composed in 1765:

In the barbaric centuries of the West, [philosophy] was nothing but an absurd and senseless jargon sanctified by fanaticism and worshipped out of superstition . . . From the time of Aristotle until the time of Descartes, I perceive a vacuum of two thousand years.[9]

D'Alembert put forward a similar view in his Preface to the *Encyclopedia*:

Descartes at least had the courage to show good thinkers how to shake off the yoke of scholasticism, of opinion, of authority – in a word, of prejudice and barbarism; and by this revolt, whose fruits we are gathering today, he did Philosophy a service, more difficult perhaps than any of those done by his illustrious successors. He can be regarded as the leader of a conspiracy, the one who had the courage to rise up first against a despotic and arbitrary power.

But there is something grudging about d'Alembert's praise. Like many other enlightenment thinkers, he believed that

Descartes was dwarfed by Newton. It was Newton, not

---

*I beg posterity never to believe anything attributed to me unless I have
said it myself. I am not the least bit surprised by the outlandish ideas
attributed to all the ancient philosophers whose writings have come down
to us; but since they were amongst the best minds of their time, I do not
believe that their ideas can really have been all that absurd, but only that
they have been misrepresented.*

Descartes[10]

Descartes, who had 'cast philosophy in a form which it seems
that it must retain for ever'.[11]

The process by which Newton replaced Descartes as the hero
of the 'new philosophy' was very gradual. The early English
scientific establishment, represented by thinkers like Locke,
Boyle, Hooke and Glanville, was lavish in its admiration for
Descartes.[12] Boyle, for example, regarded Descartes as 'the
most acute modern philosopher'.[13] Newton's works were of
course held in very high esteem; but his main work, the
Principia, which came out in Latin in 1686, was extremely
difficult, and was not adequately translated into English until
1729. For many years, Newtonian physics was normally
treated as little more than a commentary on Cartesianism. In
1671 Rohault's *Traité de Physique* was published in Paris. This
was the most important of the many books on Cartesian
physics published in the seventeenth century. It was translated
into Latin in 1697, by Newton's friend and disciple, Samuel
Clarke. In this form, Rohault's book was used in many
English and American colleges. Newton's work became
generally known through the appendices to Clarke's translation, which were expanded as further editions were produced,
rather than through Newton's own writings. Clarke's edition
of Rohault was still used as a textbook at Newton's university,
Cambridge, as late as 1730.[14]

Even though Newton's influence made itself felt only
gradually, it was clear to most scientists that his physical theory
was vastly superior to that of Descartes. This made Descartes's
confidence that his own physical theory reflected the true

nature of the physical world seem unjustified. In particular, the basic Newtonian concept of gravity did not fit in with the reductive, mechanistic, ideal of scientific explanation to which Descartes was committed (see above, p.54). So a need for retrenchment was felt; there was a retreat from the optimistic humanism of Descartes's theory of knowledge. Locke was one of the first to express this mood. His *Essay Concerning Human Understanding* (1690) expressed a resigned pessimism about the possibility of 'certain knowledge of universal truths concerning natural bodies'. Locke criticized Descartes by saying, 'It becomes the modesty of philosophy not to pronounce magisterially, where we want that evidence that can produce knowledge.'[15] Similarly, Fontenelle spoke of Cartesianism 'soaring up audaciously' while Newtonian theory was 'more timid and modest'.[16] This resignation was taken over by the scientists and philosophers of the enlightenment. D'Alembert asked, 'What difference does it make to us fundamentally whether or not we penetrate to the essence of bodies?'[17] and the Dutch physicist, s'Gravesande, said, 'We simply do not know whether these laws (i.e. the laws of nature) are derived from the nature of matter.'[18]

Descartes's humanism about knowledge and his confidence in his physics were out of keeping with this modest and sceptical climate of opinion. As a result, Descartes was seen as a builder of fanciful systems, a dreamer and a fanatic. Voltaire saw Newton and Descartes as representatives of totally opposed intellectual outlooks, and even insinuated that Newton's was essentially progressive, whereas Descartes's was essentially

---

No one but a Cartesian accuses others of Cartesianism.

Pascal[19]

---

reactionary. Descartes, he said, was 'possessed by the desire to establish a system'.[20] As this attitude to Descartes became standard, it came to be believed that Cartesian physics was nothing but a fantastic theoretical contraption appended to a wildly undisciplined speculative theology. For example, one enthusiastic Newtonian wrote in 1750: 'There never was, perhaps, a more extravagant undertaking than such an attempt, [as Descartes's] to deduce, by necessary consequences, the whole fabric of nature, and a full explication of her phaeno-mena, from any ideas we are able to form of an infinitely perfect being.'[21] The verdict of the enlightenment on Descartes was summed up by Condillac when he praised Newton for being the author of 'a project less handsome, or rather less daring, than that of Descartes, but wiser'.[22]

Since the eighteenth century, histories of philosophy have tended to classify philosophers into opposing 'schools', which are supposed to have agreed about what the basic problems of philosophy are, but to have proposed opposite solutions to them. As a result, the possibility that in the course of history philosophers have contributed to a progressive enlargement of theoretical understanding has been completely lost from sight.

The modern image of Descartes is a product of this general view of the history of philosophy. Newton and Descartes have come to be seen as representatives of quite opposite schools of thought. The Newtonian school, often referred to as 'empiri-cism', is supposed to hold that scientific knowledge is obtained only by the patient and painstaking collection of facts; and the Cartesian school, often referred to as 'rationalism' or 'a priorism', is supposed to have tried to skip this hard work and to dream up pleasing theories based on whimsical generalities.

The writer of a history of philosophy has to interpret not so much the personality of the philosopher, even his intellectual personality, as the focus and form of his system, and even less to dwell on psychological minutiae and subtleties; he has rather to separate what is definite, the permanent and genuine crystallisations from the proofs, the debating points and the philosopher's own presentation, in so far as these are self-conscious; he has to separate the ever advancing progress of true philo-sophical knowledge from the wordy exterior consciousness of the subject, a progress which manifests itself in so many forms and is the stuff and energy of those developments.

Karl Marx[23]

Modern historians of science, even if they acknowledge that Descartes made extremely important contributions to science, tend to present him as an example of 'the ambitious scientist hoping to get from his own head and from a few *a priori* principles the whole of science'.[24] And a typical historian of philosophy says of Descartes that in the field of science 'no real discovery of any kind stands to his credit', and says that in Descartes's theory of science, 'physical existence ceases to be relevant: what matters is conformity to mathematical type. Actuality yields to possibility, fact to formula, and we are embarked on the fatal sea of the *a priori*.'[25] This modern image of Descartes has almost completely obliterated the old view that he was the founder of the 'new philosophy', whose work was carried on by Newton and later scientists; but it is the old view which is closest to the truth. The principles of the 'new philosophy', and the theory of knowledge and the theory of human nature which go with it; the concepts of an idea, of mathematical laws of nature, and of a world which is not supervised by a personal God, are so fundamental to modern consciousness that it is hard not to regard them as part of the natural property of the human mind. But, in fact, they are a product of the seventeenth century, and above all of the work of Descartes.

[APPENDIX 1]

Simple Natures

In the Sixth Rule there is a crucial passage about absolutes and relatives:

> Whatever contains the pure and simple nature which we seek to know [*naturam puram et simplicem de qua est quaestio*] is known as 'absolute'. This means whatever we consider as independent, a cause, simple, universal, one, equal, similar straight, etc. . . . On the other hand, the relative [*respectivum*] is what participates in this same nature, or at least has enough in common with it for it to be referred to the absolute, and so deduced from it in several steps; but over and above this it involves others things in its concept [*in suo conceptu involvit*], which I call *respectus*. The relative is [*tale est*] whatever is said to be dependent, an effect, composite, multiple, unequal, dissimilar, curved, etc.[1]

Unfortunately, this passage has been widely misinterpreted. No one working with the standard English translations can be blamed for this, however. Both Haldane and Ross and Kemp Smith translate both '*respectus*' and '*respectivum*' as 'relative', thereby obscuring an important distinction. And they both make it appear that the list of criteria of relativeness applies to the 'other things involved' in the absolute – i.e. to the *respectus*, which cannot be correct since '*respectus*' is plural and '*tale*' singular.

Both translators are also misleading about the Rule itself, which mentions the necessity of sorting out the very simplest things from ones which are more involved (*involutis*). But instead of putting 'involved' they both put 'complex' (which they use elsewhere to translate '*compositus*' which I translate 'composite'). Thus they give the impression that the purpose of the Sixth Rule is to explain the difference between simple and composite natures.

In fact, however, the purpose of the Rule is to explain the

difference between absolutes and relatives; and it must be a mistake to identify this difference with the difference between simple and composite natures, for two reasons. First, the quoted passage says that absolutes contain simple natures; it does not say they can be identified with them. Nor can composite natures be identified with relatives, since relatives may involve *respectus*, which, unlike composite natures, cannot be 'deduced from' simple natures. (One might say that the *respectus* do not have natures at all.) Second, the notion of absolutes is relative in a way that the notion of simple natures is not. Descartes says that 'some things are from one point of view more absolute than others, but from another more relative'.[2] This could not possibly apply to simple and composite natures; the idea of reducing the one to the other would be senseless if their relationship was as ambiguous as this. Therefore it must be a mistake to identify the absolutes with the simple natures and the relatives with the composite natures.

Many authors who make this mistake combine it with another. They not only identify the simple natures with the absolutes, but also mistake the list of criteria of absolutes for a list of examples. The consequence of this double mistake is that they end up treating the *criteria of absoluteness* as *examples of simple natures*. Beck, for example, in his study of the *Rules*, criticizes commentators who ignore the 'list of examples of simple natures, given in Rule Six' and instead 'take the easier road of discussing the doctrine in terms of its formulation in Rule Twelve alone'. But as he sets off on the difficult road, Beck, not surprisingly, gets nervous. 'It must be admitted,' he remarks, 'that the discussions in *Regulae* which treat of the simple natures are not amongst the simplest texts of Descartes.' The conclusions Beck reaches are indeed puzzling. 'The characteristics of being "independent", of being "a cause" or "simple", "universal", "one", "equal", "like", "straight" . . . are all described as simple natures,' he says.[3] One may well wonder how Descartes hoped to advance scientific knowledge by saying it should reduce everything to these.[4]

Another misconception about the simple natures deserves

mention. It is often noticed that Descartes's procedure in the *First Meditation* has some connection with the theory of absolutes as expounded in Rule XII. In the course of applying the method of doubt to various ranges of things, Descartes remarks: 'We have to admit that there are certain things more simple and universal, out of which, as out of real colours, all these images of things in our minds (*cogitatione*) – whether true or false – are composed (*effinguntur*).'[5] Though Descartes gives as examples of these simples, the general nature of matter, its extension, the shapes of extended things, their quantity (i.e. magnitude and number), their location and duration, certain readers have battened on to the analogy of 'real colours' and suggested that *these* are examples of simple natures. But it is clear that Descartes mentions 'real colours' simply as an analogy for, not as an example of, simple natures; and this is confirmed by the fact that he uses the same analogy in the *Rules*.[6]

The standard criticisms of Descartes's Argument for the Existence of God

I. Most treatments of the ontological argument suggest that it involves a simple logical blunder. The usual criticisms anticipate or derive from the Kantian view that logical relations hold only between predicates, and that in this sense existence is not a predicate.[1] It follows directly from this view that any argument is invalid if it purports to give a proof of something's existence purely on the basis of logical relations.[2]

Such criticisms may seem question-begging, because Descartes's argument is precisely that in one and only one case there *is* a logical relation between a predicate and existence. But thanks to the work of modern logicians, they can now be made to appear powerful. Russell, following Frege, constructed an artificial language in which the concept of existence was represented by a symbolic apparatus with a distinctive structure, namely, the apparatus of instantial or existential quantification. It is widely believed that when Descartes's argument is translated into this artificial language, its fallaciousness becomes immediately apparent. This belief has been expressed by G. E. M. Anscombe:

According to the ontological argument, the notion of God involves that of existence, as that of a triangle involves the various properties of a triangle; therefore, God exists. Let us concede the premise ... The premise should be stated as follows: Just as *if* anything is a triangle, it has those properties, so *if* anything is God, it must possess eternal existence. This is fair ...

But, according to Anscombe, this does not prove that God exists.

For, quite generally, from: 'For all x, if φx, then ψx' we cannot infer: 'There is an x such that φx.' That is, interpreting 'φx' as 'x is

God' and 'ψx' as 'x has eternal existence', we cannot infer '*There is
a God*' from 'For all x, if x is God, x has eternal existence.' We can
very well grant that and still ask 'But *is* there such a being?' We
may well say: 'It belongs to the concept of a phoenix never to die,
but eternally to renew its life in the flames'; but we cannot infer from
the concept that there lives such a creature.[3]

This criticism is not conclusive. Beginning as it does with the
phrase 'quite generally', and ending with an example which
presupposes that the concept of a phoenix was relevantly
similar to that of God, it invites the reply that this attempt to
translate Descartes's argument into the artificial language
created by Russell is a failure, because it does not do justice to
Descartes's view that the concept of God is quite unique in
involving existence. The question to be asked about Descartes's
argument is not so much Anscombe's question, 'But *is* there
such a being?', as the question 'Is there such a concept, and if
so is it really a concept of God?' (see above, pp. 139-140).

II. Another general criticism of Descartes's attempt to argue
from the concept of God to the existence of God has recently
been put forward by Anthony Kenny,[4] who says that
Descartes's argument is implicitly Meinongian. Meinongism,
for these purposes, can be defined as the view that there are at
least two types of existence. One of them, a very general one,
sometimes called 'secondary existence', belongs both to what is
possible and to what is actual; the other, 'primary existence',
applies only to what is actual. According to Kenny, Descartes
was arguing from God's having secondary existence to his
having primary existence; and this argument has to be rejected
because Meinongism has to be rejected.[5]

As an interpretation of Descartes, this is implausible, since
Descartes never made any explicitly Meinongian statements,
and indeed Descartes's rejection of 'universals' (see above, pp.
38, 86) seems to involve a rejection of Meinongism. Moreover it is hard to see the point of Meinongism, as Kenny
interprets it, either in general or in relation to Descartes's
arguments for the existence of God. Descartes certainly

presupposes that it makes sense to investigate the content, meaning or 'objective reality' of an idea without thereby directly committing oneself to the claim that anything in the world corresponds to the idea. For instance, he thought one could prove theorems about triangles without committing oneself to the actual existence of triangles. This procedure is perfectly normal and acceptable. And he thought one could try to do the same with the concept of God; one could try to set aside the question of God's existence and just investigate the concept of God. But he thought that investigation of this concept, unlike the investigation of any other, would reveal that what it represented actually exists. His analysis of the concept of God is neither more nor less Meinongian than the perfectly normal and acceptable procedure of analysing the concept of a triangle.[6]

Notes

INTRODUCTION

1 Letter to Mersenne, iv, 34.
2 Adrien Baillet, *Vie de M. Descartes* (1691), vol. II, p. 515.
3 *Discourse on Method* VI, AT VI 61; HR I 119.

I SCIENCE AND PHILOSOPHY

1 Letter to Beeckmann, 26 iii 19.
2 Cf. Henri Gouhier, *Les Premières Pensées de Descartes*, pp. 46–7; Gaston Milhaud, *Descartes Savant*, ch. 2, esp. p. 49.
3 *Olympica*, AT X 179. Baillet, *Vie de M. Descartes*, vol. I, p. 51.
4 Baillet, op. cit., vol. I, pp. 163–5. A translation of this passage is available in Norman Kemp Smith, *New Studies in the Philosophy of Descartes*, pp. 42–5.
5 *Discourse*, title page.
6 *Discourse* VI, AT VI 62; HR I 119.
7 *Rules for the Direction of the Mind* V, AT X 380; HR I 14.
8 According to Kemp Smith, 'His metaphysical teaching is perverted ... by principles wholly at variance with his positive scientific views' (*Studies in the Cartesian Philosophy*, pp. v–vi).
9 The classical statement of this *atomistic* aspect of empiricism was made by David Hume (1711–76), who tried to analyse causation in terms of the 'links' or 'connections' between things, but expressed doubts about whether people can ever really know that such 'links' or 'connections' exist. Hume's main discussion of cause is in his *Treatise on Human Nature*, I iii 1–3.
10 *Rules* VI, AT X 383, HR I 16.
11 In the *Meteors*, he showed that they were caused by a combination of refraction and reflection of light in water droplets.
12 *Principia Ethica*, Cambridge University Press, 1903, p. 135.
13 *Two Great Systems* (1632), Third Day, Salusbury Translation, 1661, p. 301. Quoted in Burtt's *Metaphysical Foundations of Modern Physical Science*, p. 69. In this passage Galileo links the name of the ancient Greek scientist Aristarchus with that of Copernicus. For a more modern translation see pp. 327–8 of Drake's edition.
14 *Capital*, vol. III, ch. 48, p. 817.
15 Letter to Mersenne, iii 36.

16 ibid., iii 37; cf. letter to Vatier, 22 ii 38; to ********, 27 iv 37 (?).
The explanation of the method in the *Discourse* is indeed very baffling.
It is summarized in four brief rules (*Discourse* II, AT VI 18–19; HR I 92)
which seem so platitudinous that there is some justice in Leibniz's
rude summary of them: 'Take what you need, and operate on it
as you should, and you will have what you want' (Gerhardt, vol. IV,
p. 329).

17 But parts of it were published in the Port Royal *Logic* (1662), and Leibniz
and, possibly, Locke saw it before it was published. See. S. V. Keeling,
Descartes, p. 13.

18 *Rules* XVI, AT X 454; HR I 66.

19 Most translators speak of 'complex natures' instead of 'composite
natures'. This is a confusing habit, because it wrongly suggests a parallel
between Descartes's distinction, which is essentially scientific, and
Locke's distinction between simple and complex ideas, which is essentially epistemological. Descartes's word is '*compositus*', though he
mentions '*complexus*' as a possible alternative (*Rules* VIII, AT X 399;
HR I 27).

20 'There is nothing to science (*humanam scientiam*) apart from seeing distinctly (*distincte*) how the simple natures run together to compose other
things'; *Rules* XII, AT X 427; HRI 46. Descartes sometimes speaks of the
simple nature as the 'cause' of the composite nature, and of the one as
deducible from the other.

21 *Rules* XII, AT X 419; HR I 41.

22 'There are no simple natures which are not either mental or physical or
both'; *Rules* VIII, AT X 399; HR I 27.

23 *Sophist* 218D–221C.

24 Letter to Regius, v 41.

2 MATHEMATICS

1 J. S. Mill, *An Examination of Sir William Hamilton's Philosophy*, p. 617;
cited in D. E. Smith, *History of Mathematics*, New York, Dover, 1958,
vol. I, p. 375.

2 'Thomas Hobbes', *Brief Lives*,

3 Letter to Mersenne, xii 37.

4 This was recorded by Beeckmann in 1628. See AT X 331.

5 Something very like it had been developed by Oresme in the fourteenth
century; and in any case it was only an elaboration of ancient Greek
techniques. See Milhaud, *Descartes Savant*, pp. 34, 140.

6 If it had seemed an important discovery then, as Milhaud points out, it
would almost certainly have become a matter of disputed precedence
between Descartes and Fermat. They disputed precedence in other
things with less reason. ibid., p. 140.

7 'It seems to me to be precisely this science (true mathematics) which has been given the barbaric name of "algebra".' *Rules* IV, AT X 377; HR I 12. Cf. L. Liard, 'Méthode et mathématique de Descartes', *Revue Philosophique*, 10, 1880, pp. 569–600, esp. p. 591. Cf. also Jacques Vuillemin, *Mathématiques et métaphysique chez Descartes*, pp. 64, 87.

8 Cf. Smith, loc. cit.

9 *Rules* XIV, AT X 440–41; HR I 56.

10 ibid., AT X 442; HR I 57.

11 'Show me the geometer who does not ruin the obviousness of his subject with incoherent principles (*repugnantibus principiis*) – by saying lines have no breadth, and surfaces no depth, and then constructing the one from the other, without noticing that a line whose movement is to generate a surface must be a real physical object (*verum corpus*)'; *Rules* XIV, AT X 446; HR I 60.

12 Descartes continues: 'I could find nothing simpler, and nothing which could be presented more distinctly to my imagination or my senses.' *Discourse* II, AT VI 20; HR I 93. The word corresponding to 'straight' occurs only in the Latin translation, which was supervised by Descartes. Cf. Milhaud, op. cit., p. 70.

13 *Discourse* II, AT VI 20; HR I 93.

14 'René Descartes', *Brief Lives*.

15 *Rules* IV, AT X 377; HR I 12.

16 Cf. L. Millet, 'Descartes et le symbolisme algébrique', *Les Études Philosophiques*, 1956, pp. 263–86, esp. p. 265.

17 See Beeckmann's journal, AT X 334. Cf. Milhaud, op. cit., p. 72n.

18 '*Facilius mentibus insinuantur*'; these are the words in which Beeckmann reported the discovery, AT X 333.

19 'When I speak of a^2, b^2 etc., I do not ordinarily mean anything but simple lines; though in order to follow normal usage in algebra, I call them squares or cubes.' *Geometry* I, AT VI 371. See also *Rules* XIV–XV, AT X 450–54; HR I 63–8.

20 *Rules* XVIII, AT X 461–8; HR I 71–7. Cf. Milhaud, op. cit., p. 73; Vuillemin, op. cit., pp. 72–3.

21 'I hope to demonstrate in the realm of continuous quantity, that some problems can be solved using only straight lines and circles, while others require various curves, generated by a single movement, which can be produced by a new type of compasses'; letter to Beeckmann, 26 iii 19; AT X 157. The instrument is described in *Geometry* II, AT VI 391–2. Descartes wrote, 'I do not want to undertake to change names whose usage is settled; but it seems obvious that as we take for geometrical that which is precise and exact, and for mechanical that which is not, and considering geometry as the science which teaches the measurement of all bodies, one should no more exclude the more complex (*composées*)

lines than the simplest ones, as long as one can imagine (*imaginer*) them described by a single movement, or by several successive ones where the later ones are completely determined by the earlier ones; for in this way one can always know their measurement exactly.' *Geometry* II, AT VI 389-90.

22 In particular he thought the spiral and the quadratrix 'belong only to mechanics'; *Geometry* II, AT VI 390.

23 Letter to Arnauld, 14 iii 1686. Gerhardt, vol. II, p. 61; *Discourse on Metaphysics* VI, Gerhardt, vol. IV, p. 431.

24 Cf. *Discourse* I, AT VI 7; HR I 85.

25 *Passions*, Preface, AT XI 314-15, 316. This is not translated by HR.

26 'No other principles are required in physics than are used in Geometry or Abstract Mathematics, nor should any be desired, for all natural phenomena are explained by them.' *Principles* II 64 title, AT VIII 78; HR I 269. Cf. *Rules* IV, AT X 377-8; HR I 12-13; *Meditations* V, AT VII 65; AT IX 52; HR I 180.

27 *Discourse* II, AT VI 18; HR I 92. In *Rules* IV (AT X 377; HR I 13) Descartes says that his mathematics was distilled from geometry, arithmetic, astronomy, music, optics and mechanics. This curious list is partly explained by the fact that the Pythagoreans had divided mathematics into arithmetic (number theory), geometry, music and astronomy. They regarded music as applied arithmetic and astronomy as applied geometry. This classification was incorporated into medieval university syllabuses as part of the quadrivium.

28 *Discourse*, title page.

29 This law was discovered independently by Snell in 1621 and is known as Snell's Law. The date of Descartes's discovery is generally believed to be 1626. Cf. A. I. Sabra, *Theories of Light from Descartes to Newton*, p. 102.

30 Letter to Mersenne, xii 37.

31 'It is demanding the impossible to require geometrical demonstrations of me in questions of physics'; letter to Mersenne, 17 v 38.

32 The main place where he used it is the appendix to the *Replies* to the second set of *Objections* (AT VII 160-70; AT IX 124-32; HR II 52-9). There may also have been an early work in this style on the pressures of fluids in vessels (Milhaud, op. cit., p. 34). Descartes could not have claimed any originality for the use he made of the 'geometrical method'. The method was used in ancient mathematics, and its use had been extended to non-mathematical subject matters in the twelfth century, by Nicolas of Amiens in his *Ars Catholicae Fidei* (cf. Étienne Gilson, *La Philosophie au Moyen Age*, pp. 77-8).

33 Important examples of the mistaken criticism of Descartes for being wedded to the 'geometrical' method are: Edmund Husserl, *Cartesian Meditations*, p. 7; O. Hamelin, *Le Système de Descartes*, p. 34; Pierre

Duhem, *The Aim and Structure of Physical Theory*, Princeton, N.J., Princeton University Press, 1954, p. 65; and recently Rom Harré, *Principles of Scientific Thinking*, Macmillan, 1970, pp. 8–10.

34 The notions of axioms and postulates were so ill defined that there would have been nothing to stop one making a theory 'geometrical' simply by calling each of the sentences in which it was expressed an axiom or a postulate.

35 Leibniz wrote the propaganda on behalf of the Count Palatine, Philip William of Neuberg, who was a candidate for the Polish throne. The propaganda was unsuccessful. See H. W. Carr, *Leibniz*, Constable, 1929, p. 11.

36 *Rules* IV, AT X 377–8; HR I 13.

37 *Rules* XIV, AT X 447; HR I 61.

38 Cf. B. Gibson, 'The *Regulae* of Descartes', *Mind*, 1898, p. 359.

39 Cf. J. F. Scott, *The Scientific Work of René Descartes*, pp. 93–4. Thus where Stevinus, writing in 1585, would have written:
$$3(2) - 5(1) + 6(.) = 0$$
and where Vieta, writing in 1594, would have written:
$$3 \text{ in A quad} - 5 \text{ in A plane} + 6 \text{ aequatur } 0$$
Descartes would write:
$$3x^2 - 5x + 6 = 0$$
Cf. L. Hogben, *Mathematics for the Million*, revised edition, Pan Books, 1967, p. 259.

40 *Rules* XVI, AT X 456, 458; HR I 67–8, 69.

41 Leibniz hit on an idea which fits this conception of science very neatly. He proposed that simple ideas should be represented by prime numbers, and complex ones by the products of primes. The derivation of complex terms from simple ones could then be seen at a glance, since there is only one way of decomposing any natural number into primes. Cf. Gerhardt, vol. VII, p. 292. See W. and M. Kneale, *The Development of Logic*, Oxford University Press, 1962, p. 329.

3 METHOD

1 *Rules* XII, AT X 426; HR I 47.

2 See Jonathan Rée, 'Descartes' Method', unpublished B.Phil. thesis, Oxford University, 1972.

3 *Meno* 86B–87A.

4 *Replies* II, AT VII 155; AT IX 121–2; HR II 49.

5 Cf. Galileo, *Dialogues concerning the Two Chief World Systems* (1632) First Day, p. 51; Newton, *Opticks*, pp. 404–5; Leibniz, *Nouveaux Essais*, book IV, ch. 2; Gerhardt, vol. VII, pp. 349–50; see also Kant, *Prolegomena to any Future Metaphysics*, p. 23; Dijksterhuis, *The Mechanisation of the World Picture*, pp. 235, 339; G. Buchdahl, *Metaphysics and the Philosophy*

of Science, pp. 127–9. For the use of the term in the Middle Ages, see Gilson, *La Philosophie au Moyen Age*, p. 28.

6 'This is the secret of the whole art; that in all things we should take care to see what is most absolute'; *Rules* VI, AT X 382; HR I 16. For a fuller discussion of this passage see Appendix One.

7 *Daniel Deronda*, ch. 11.

8 *The World: Treatise on Light*, AT XI 3.

9 *Discourse* VI, AT VI 63; HR I 120.

10 *Rules* VI, AT X 381; HR I 15.

11 '*Par les plus simples, on ne doit pas seulement entendre celles qui peuvent le plus aisément estre descrites, ny celles qui rendent la construction ou la démonstration du Problesme proposé plus facile, mais principalement celles qui sont du plus simple genre qui puisse déterminer la quantité qui est cherchée*'; *Geometry* III, AT VI 442.

12 Descartes's use of this terminology antedates his discovery of co-ordinate geometry. See, for example, his letter to Beeckmann, 26 iii 19, AT X 157.

13 *The World: Treatise on Light* II, AT XI 10.

14 Cf. *Rules* XII, AT X 413; HR I 37, where Descartes advises an inquirer into colours to represent different colours by means of 'similar' diagrams.

15 'Universals are involved whenever several things are to be thought of under one and the same idea. If we give one name to all these things, it is a universal name . . . Number and all universals are only modes of thought (*modi cogitandi*)'; *Principles* I 49, 48.

16 In his commentary on Descartes, Spinoza says that Descartes 'considered all universals, such as material nature in general, and its extent, likewise shape, quantity, and so on'; *Opera*, vol. IV, p. 111.

17 *Novum Organon*, II 29.

18 Letter to Mersenne, 23 xii 30, AT II 380.

19 *Discourse* VI, AT VI 63; HR I 120.

20 Galileo, according to Descartes, used to 'seek the reasons for various particular effects without having considered the first causes of nature'; letter to Mersenne, 11 x 38.

21 Fermat, according to Descartes, had discovered 'many beautiful things' but he failed to 'study things in a very general way, so as to arrive at rules which also apply to other fields'; letter to Schooten, quoted in Milhaud, *Descartes Savant*, p. 183.

22 *Two New Sciences* (1638), translated by H. Crew and A. de Salvio, p. 255; *Two Chief Systems* (1632), translated by S. Drake, p. 29.

23 *The Search After Truth*, AT X 515–16; HR I 317.

24 *Encyclopédie*, Discours Préliminaire, p. vi.

25 *Principles* IV 203, French only. The difference between Descartes's approach to classification and the method of division is discussed, very

briefly, by Alan Gewirth in 'Clearness and Distinctness in Descartes', *Philosophy*, 1943, n. 73. Reprinted in Doney (ed.), *Descartes*, p. 273.

26 Descartes's criticisms have been thoroughly criticized by Étienne Gilson in his *Études sur le rôle de la pensée médiévale dans la formation du système Cartésien*, especially p. 163.

27 'Knowledge of the aim does not provide knowledge of the nature of the thing itself; the nature of the thing remains quite hidden. This is Aristotle's chief failing'; *Interview with Burman*, AT V 158.

28 Descartes explained how he saw the role of purpose in God's creation of the world in his letter to Chanut, vi 47.

29 The movement was led by thinkers like Ramus (1515–72) and Telesio (1509–88).

30 On occult properties, see Dijksterhuis, op. cit., p. 157.

31 *Principles* IV 187; cf. letter to Morin, 13 vii 38.

32 For instance he sought a rich philanthropist to finance a 'description (*histoire*) of celestial appearances ... without reasons or hypotheses'; letter to Mersenne, 10 v 32; cf. letter to Mersenne, 25 xii 30.

33 *Discourse* VI, AT VI 75; HR I 128.

34 J. F. Scott, *The Scientific Work of René Descartes*, p. 164.

35 An exception which proves this rule is Descartes's letter to Plempius, 23 iii 38, which describes in detail the experiments Descartes did with eels' hearts.

36 For example, Descartes was convinced, quite wrongly, that light travels instantaneously. He wrote, 'If it should be proved false I should be ready to confess that I know absolutely nothing in philosophy' (letter to Beeckmann, 22 viii 34). However it is possible that what Descartes meant was that light does not travel as an emission of particles. See A. I. Sabra, *Theories of Light*, p. 50; cf. J. F. Scott, op. cit., p. 40.

37 For example, Newton's famous experiment with two prisms, which he thought proved the heterogeneity of white light, did not in fact do so (A. I. Sabra, op. cit., pp. 249–50).

38 Dijksterhuis, op. cit., p. 269.

39 'Rules of Reasoning in Philosophy, III', *Principia* (1686), p. 398.

40 *Opticks*, p. 401.

41 ibid., pp. 404–5.

42 *Origins of Forms and Qualities*, Preface, *Works*, vol. III, p. 13.

4 PHYSICS

1 By Henri Renier (Reneri); cf. Paul Mouy, *Le Développement de la Physique Cartésienne*, p. 9.

2 *The World*, AT XI 26; cf. *Principles* IV 188.

3 *Gospel According to St Mark*, v:30.

4 'Otherwise I cannot understand how the application of the Sun and

Moon to the Earth to effect production should be any other than to lay a marble statue in the chamber of the bride and from that conjunction to expect children'; *Dialogue on Two Great Systems* (Salusbury Translation). For a more modern translation, see Drake's edition, p. 60.

5 Things which do not have quantities, such as spatial positions, are neither substantial nor insubstantial.

6 *Rules* XII, AT X 418; HR I 40–41. Cf. *Rules* XII, AT X 420; HR I 42: 'This way of representing things will allow us to claim later that everything we can know is composed (*composita*) of simple natures: for instance, if I judge that a certain shape is not moving, I will say that the thought (*cogitationem*) I have of it is composed (*compositam*) of shape and rest; and similarly for other things.'

7 An analogy used by Leibniz, who attributes it to Rohault. See *Nouveaux Essais*, book II, ch. 23, para. 28, Gerhardt, vol. V, p. 208.

8 Voltaire, *Élémens de la Philosophie de Newton*, part I, ch. 1, para. 5; *Œuvres XXII*, p. 404 (not in the 1738 edition).

9 *The World* III, AT XI 11. On Occam's earlier attempt to treat motion as something like a substance, see J. A. Weisheipl, *The Development of Physical Theory in the Middle Ages*, p. 67.

10 Cf. Leibniz's reference to the 'two great laws of nature, that of force and that of direction'; to Arnauld 30 iv 87, Gerhardt, vol. IX, p. 94.

11 *The World* VII, AT XI 38; cf. *Principles* II 37.

12 ibid., 41; cf. *Principles* II 40.

13 ibid., 43–4; cf. *Principles* II 34.

14 *Dialogues concerning Two New Sciences*, translated by H. Crew and A. de Salvio, p. 215.

15 Cf. A. Koyré, 'Galilée et la loi d'inertie', esp. appendix B, *Études Galiléennes*, part III. See also ibid., part II: 'La loi de la chute des corps', p. 108. See also Alan Gabbey, 'Force and Inertia in Seventeenth-Century Dynamics', *Studies in History and Philosophy of Science*, II, May 1971, p. 61.

16 *Principles* II 25.

17 'Although motion is no more than a mode of this matter which is moved there is, nevertheless, a certain determinate quantity of it, which never increases or diminishes, though in particular bodies there is sometimes more of it and sometimes less'; *Principles* II 36.

18 Letter to More, 30 viii 49.

19 *Principles* II 28.

20 Cf. Newton, *Principia Mathematica*, book I, Scholium to Definitions, pp. 6–12.

21 *The World* VI, AT XI 36. It is not clear who was supposed to believe that extension was an 'accident'.

22 Cf. *Principles* II 17.

23 Voltaire, for example, argued as follows: 'Those who cannot conceive

of a vacuum, make the objection that a vacuum would be nothing, that nothing can have no properties, and that therefore nothing would operate in a vacuum. The answer is that it is not the case that a vacuum is nothing: it is the place of bodies, it is space, it has properties, it is extended in length, breadth, and depth, it is penetrable, inseparable etc.' *Élémens de la Philosophie de Newton*, p. 210.

24 *The World* IV, AT XI 19.
25 ibid., 44, 19.
26 ibid., 20.
27 *Principles* II 34.
28 *Replies* VI, AT VII 441; AT IX 240; HR II 255.
29 People who postulated gravity as an irreducible property of matter 'assumed some principle which they have not completely understood'. They 'do not know the nature of what we call gravity', *Principles*, letter to translator, AT IX (ii) 7–8; HR I 207. Descartes singled out his explanation of gravity for special mention in the summary of *The World* in the *Discourse on Method*, AT VI 44; HR I 108.
30 Cf. *Principia*, book II, propositions LI, LII, LIII and Scholia, pp. 385–396. See also Cotes's Preface to second edition, 1713, xxviii–xxxi.
31 Cotes, Preface to second edition, p. xxvi.
32 *Opticks*, second edition (1717), p. 376.
33 Letter to Bentley, 1693; cited in Cajori's Appendix to Newton's *Principia*, p. 633.
34 Cited in ibid., p. 634.
35 Cf. letter to Boyle, 28 ii 1678/9, cited in ibid., p. 675 and *Opticks*, second edition, book III, part I, quest. 31, p. 376.
36 Cf. *Principia*, second edition (1713), book I, proposition LXIX, Scholium, p. 192; cf. Cajori's Appendix, p. 634, *Opticks*, second edition (1717), Advertisement II, p. cxxiii.
37 Since momentum is a product of rate of movement and quantity of matter, the concept of rate of movement must be different from that of momentum. But Descartes never showed any clear understanding of the difference – perhaps because he was committed to saying that conservation principles apply to every one of them. Obviously if conservation principles apply to two of these quantities, a conservation principle must apply to the third too.
38 Leibniz defined momentum as mass times the square of velocity, rather than mass times velocity (the definition used by Descartes and Newton). Leibniz's definition is a definition of energy rather than momentum. See Leibniz's *Discourse on Metaphysics* XVII; cf. Buchdahl, *Metaphysics and the Philosophy of Science*, pp. 148ff.
39 Energy is mass times the square of velocity, and unlike momentum is not a vectoral quantity. Descartes's concept of momentum seems to combine some of the features of the modern concept of momentum with some

of the features of the concept of energy; cf. Dominic Dubarle, 'Sur la notion de quantité de mouvement', p. 118.

40 *The World* III, AT XI 15.
41 *Principles* II 53.
42 *Principles* II 11.
43 *Principles* II 46–52; cf. R. J. Blackwell, 'Descartes' Laws of Motion', esp. pp. 227–8.
44 *Principles* II 53.
45 Cf. Herivel, *The Background to Newton's* Principia, p. 42.
46 Newton inscribed his copy of Descartes's *Geometry* with the remark '*Error, error, non est geom.*'
47 Cf. A. Koyré, *Metaphysics and Measurement*, ch. I.
48 *The Mechanisation of the World Picture*, p. 30.
49 De la Forge, *Traité de l'Espirt de l'Homme*, ch. XVI; cited in Norman Kemp Smith, *Studies in the Cartesian Philosophy*, pp. 76–7.
50 'Newtonian mechanics, for example, imposes a unified form of description on the world . . . The possibility of describing the world by means of Newtonian mechanics tells us nothing about the world'; Wittgenstein, *Tractatus Logico-Philosophicus* 6.341, 6.342. 'The unification of all laws in the concept of universal Attraction expresses no further content than just the bare concept of the law itself, a concept which is therein set down as existing'; Hegel, *Phenomenology of Mind*, translated by J.B. Baillie, Unwin, 1910, p. 196. See also G. Frege, 'On the Law of Inertia', 1891, translated in *Studies in History and Philosophy of Science*, 1971.
51 *The World* VII, AT XI 43.
52 ibid.; cf. *Principles* II 36.
53 *The World* III, AT XI 11.

5 DESCARTES'S EARLY CONCEPT OF IDEAS

1 According to A. R. Hall, 'This concept of Descartes' is the most fecund in the history of biology' (*From Galileo to Newton* (1963), Fontana, 1970, p. 198).
2 The exact location of the centre of the nervous system was specified in the *Treatise on Man* (cf. AT XI 129, 131–2, 146ff.) but not in the earlier work, the *Rules*. Descartes chose the pineal gland, because it was central and unique. Cf. *Passions* 12; letter to Britendijck, 1643(?), AT IV 62.
3 Cf. *Dioptrics* IV, AT VI 110; *The World*, AT XI 133, 142.
4 *Pensées*, 205, 206.
5 A. J. P. Kenny, 'The Homunculus Fallacy' in *Interpretations of Life and Mind*, edited by Marjorie Grene, Routledge & Kegan Paul, 1972, pp. 65–74, esp. pp. 65–6.
6 St Anselm, *Proslogion*, ch. I. Cf. Augustine's phrase, '*intravi in intima*

mea'; *Confessions* VII x 16. See H. Gouhier, *La Philosophie et son Histoire*, Paris, Vrin, 1948, p. 82.

7 *Othello*, III, iii, 112.

8 *Passions* 26.

9 I use the words 'imagination' and 'fantasy' to express two different concepts in Descartes's theory, although he himself mixed up the two words. Fantasy is one of three faculties – the others being sense and memory – which contribute information to the imagination. Descartes sometimes referred to the imagination as the *sensus communis*, although in one place he contrasts this with the imagination, saying that the former corresponds to the senses and the latter to fantasy and memory; cf. *The World*, AT XI 176–7.

10 The *Dioptrics*, though published in 1637, was written about 1628–31.

11 In the *Rules* and the *Dioptrics* the word is used interchangeably with 'image', 'figure' and 'species'; cf. Kemp Smith, *New Studies*, p. 223. It is possible that Descartes was not the first to use the word 'idea' in this sense. An interesting example is to be found in a book published in France in 1622. See R. M. Blake, 'Note on the use of the term *"Idée"* prior to Descartes', *Philosophical Review*, September 1939, pp. 532–5. See also *Love's Labours Lost*, IV, ii, 69. For subsequent uses in the same sense see Hume's *Treatise*, I ii 5; Spinoza, *Ethics*, book II, 48 Scholium.

12 *The World*, AT XI 177.

13 *Rules* XIV, AT X 441; HR I 56.

14 *Richard III*, III, vii, 13.

15 A large store of information on the use of the word 'idea' is to be found in Note G of *The Works of Thomas Reid*, edited by William Hamilton, Edinburgh, 1858, pp. 925–8.

16 'It is not the mind or soul which directly moves the external members; all it can do is determine the course of this very subtle liquid, called animal spirits'; *Replies* IV, AT VII 229; AT IX 178; HR II 103.

17 (My emphasis) *The World*, AT XI 181.

18 *Dioptrics*, AT VI 141.

19 (My emphasis) *The World*, AT XI 176–7.

20 Quoted in L. L. Whyte, *The Unconscious Before Freud*, 1960, Tavistock, 1967, p. 111.

21 For example it led the author of the article on the 'Invisible' in the *Encyclopedia* to raise the question, 'Do blind people see things in their heads, or at the tips of their fingers?' It was revived by Russell, who once suggested that a neurophysiologist cannot really know about anyone's brain but his own (*The Analysis of Matter*, Kegan Paul, 1927, p. 32).

22 *Treatise*, I ii 5.

23 Cf. Wittgenstein's remark: 'Always get rid of the idea of the private object in this way: assume that it constantly changes, but that you do not

notice the change because your memory constantly deceives you' (*Philosophical Investigations* II, p. 207).

24 *Biographia Literaria*, Everyman edition, Dent, 1906, p. 70.

25 *Rules* XII, AT X 416–17; HR I 40. Descartes thought it was particularly useful to get ideas which had a geometrical similarity with what one was studying. As a result he is sometimes credited with a 'resemblance theory of meaning'. For a discussion of this interpretation, see below, 13 note 30, p. 189.

6 DOUBT AND THE SOUL

1 The theory that 1630 marks the turning-point of Descartes's thought is confirmed by his letters of that year, especially to Mersenne, 15 iv 30; and it is supported by A. Koyré, *Études Galiléennes*, p. 127; H. Gouhier, *La Pensée Métaphysique*, p. 11; F. Alquie, *La Découverte Métaphysique de l'Homme chez Descartes*, Paris, Presses Universitaires de France, 1950, part I, chs. 3 and 4.

2 Cf. H. Gouhier, 'Pour une histoire des Méditations Métaphysiques', *Revue des Sciences Humaines*, 1951, pp. 5–29.

3 Husserl's concept of *époché*, though it claims Cartesian ancestry, has in fact comparatively little in common with Descartes's method of doubt.

4 It is pointed out that the occurrence of psychological verbs like 'doubt' (or 'conceive') creates opaque or intensional contexts; cf. Geach, *God and the Soul*, p. 7; Kenny, *Descartes*, p. 80.

5 *Objections* IV, AT VII 202; AT IX 157–8; HR II 83–4.

6 It also draws attention to the difference between the meanings of 'it is possible to conceive of x without conceiving of y' and 'it is possible to conceive of x as existing without y'. Descartes's blindness to this difference was an important factor leading him to his invalid concept of the soul as something which might exist without the body (see above, pp. 114-117).

7 Wittgenstein, *Blue Book*, p. 25. Wittgenstein's point is used to criticize Descartes's method of doubt in John Cook's 'Human Beings' in Winch (ed.), *Studies in the Philosophy of Wittgenstein*, Routledge & Kegan Paul, 1969, pp. 134-5.

8 *Meditations*, Dedication, AT VII 3; AT IX 6; HR I 134-5.

9 *Replies* II, AT VII 156; AT IX 122; HR II 49.

10 *Discourse* I, AT VI 10; HR I 87.

11 'Several things evidently belong to this category: physical nature in general, and its extension, the shape of extended objects, their quantity – i.e. their magnitude and number – their position, their persistence through time, and so on.' *Meditations* I, AT VII 20; AT IX 16; HR I 146.

12 Cf. Descartes's remark about matter in *The World* VI, AT XI 35: 'The idea of it is included (*comprise*) in all the others which our imagination

can form in such a way that you must necessarily conceive it if you are ever to imagine anything.'

13 *Discourse* IV, AT VI 31; HR I 101.

14 *Discourse* IV, AT VI 32; HR I 101.

15 *Replies* V, AT VII 352; HR II 207.

16 In Latin, it occurred only in the *Principles* and *Replies* II, in French in the *Discourse* and the *Search After Truth*.

17 Indeed, Descartes remarked that 'it is such a simple and natural thing to infer that one exists from the fact that one is thinking that it could have occurred to any writer'; letter to (Colvius), 14 xi 40.

18 Especially in the works of Heraclitus and Aeschylus; cf. Bruno Snell, *The Discovery of the Mind*, esp. pp. 17 and 106, and E. R. Dodds, *The Greeks and the Irrational*, p. 15: 'Homeric man has no concept of what we call "soul" or "personality".'

19 Cf. J. Earle, 'A History of the word "Mind"', *Mind*, 1881, pp. 301–20.

20 *Principles of Human Knowledge* (1710), part I, para. 2. Ryle's *Concept of Mind* also fails to distinguish between the mind and the soul; see especially p. 11. It is interesting to notice that one could substitute 'mind' for 'soul' in Yeats's 'Dialogue of Self and Soul'.

21 Cf. Descartes's phrase, 'this I, that is to say, this soul, by which I am what I am'; *Discourse* IV, AT VI 33; HR I 101.

22 *Notes Against a Programme*, AT VIII 347; HR I 434.

23 *Discourse* IV, AT VI 32–3; HR I 101.

24 'Sum igitur, praecise tantum res cogitans, id est mens, sive animus, sive intellectus, sive ratio'; '... une chose qui pense, c'est à dire un esprit, un entendement, ou une raison'; *Meditations* II, AT VII 27; AT IX 21; HR I 152.

25 *Essay*, II i 19. Spinoza's attitude was quite the opposite. He found the step from the *cogito* to the identification of the soul with the mind so obvious that he remarked '"*Cogito ergo sum*" is a single (*unica*) proposition, equivalent to "I am thinking"'; *Principia Philosophiae Cartesianae*, Pars I, Prolegomenon, *Opera*, vol. IV, p. 113.

7 DESCARTES'S LATE CONCEPT OF IDEAS

1 Strictly speaking, this only applies to the Plato of the *Republic*, the *Phaedo* and other dialogues written before the *Theaetatus*.

2 *Summa Theologiae*, 1a–2ae ii 6; Gilby 624.

3 *Olympica*, AT X 217, 218, 219. These are translations of notes made by Leibniz from the original manuscript, which has not survived.

4 *Rules* XII, AT X 419; HR I 41.

5 *Rules* XIV, AT X 442–3; HR I 57.

6 Descartes failed to note that what made the piece of wax a particular, self-identical thing, was the fact that it traced a unique and continuous

path through space and time. This omission is closely related to his failure to provide a workable notion of a particle or piece of matter (see above pp. 56-57). His examination of the wax, however, was designed to reveal what was essential to something's being wax, rather than to its being a particular piece of wax. He said his argument was 'still more obvious' in relation to 'wax in general'.

7 Some readers get the mistaken impression that Descartes was advocating the 'intelligible body clothed with sensible properties' conception, because Descartes goes on to say that in ordinary language we say that we see that the wax is the same, as though this 'seeing' did not involve using our minds. Descartes tries to show how confusing this is by pointing out that we say we *see* men out of the window, even when all that meets the eye is hats and coats. 'I judge that they are real men, and so I understand, simply by the faculty of judging which is in my mind, what I believed I saw with my eyes.' Descartes's point is simply that everyone must admit that even sensible things like men may not be known directly by the senses.

8 *Opusc. XVI Exposition de Trinitate*, V 3; Gilby 54.

9 *Meditations* II, AT VII 30-32; AT IX 23-6; HR I 154-5.

10 Cf. letter to Mersenne, 16 x 39.

11 Cf. *Replies* VI, AT VII 438-9; AT IX 236; HR II 252.

12 Cf. *Discourse* VI, AT VI 36; HR I 103-4, where Descartes explains the point in terms of the possibility of thinking of triangles, and knowing theorems about them, even if one does not know that any triangles exist.

13 It seems likely that Descartes was also disingenuous in stating his reason for using the word 'idea', which I have suggested was based on its use in the sense of 'pattern' or 'copy' (see above p.65). In *Replies* III (AT VII 181; AT IX 141; HR II 68) he claims that he adapted the word from its scholastic use to mean archetypes in the mind of God.

14 Letter to Mersenne, vii 41; cf. *Replies* II, AT VII 160; AT IX 124; HR II 52. See also the important letter to Gibieuf 19 i 42; also Locke's *Essay*, Two I 1: 'Every man being conscious to himself that he thinks, and that which his mind is applied about whilst thinking being the *ideas* that are there, it is past doubt that men have in their minds several *ideas* . . .'

15 This point is asserted by Gilson, *Comm.*, p. 318. But see below, 11 note 28, p. 186.

16 *The Philosophy of the Enlightenment*, p. 38.

17 Cf. *Meditations* II, AT VII 27; AT IX 21; HR I 151-2; and *Replies* I, AT VII 116; AT IX 92; HR II 20. Cf. E. J. Ashworth, 'Descartes' theory of Clear and Distinct Ideas', in R. J. Butler (ed.), *Cartesian Studies*, Oxford, Blackwell, 1972, p. 91.

18 See *Objections and Replies* III, AT VII 179-80; AT IX 139-41; HR II 66-8.

8 IDEAS AND SCIENCE

1 Quoted in E. A. Burtt, *Metaphysical Foundations*, p. 68.
2 *Dialogue on the Great World Systems* (1632) First Day. See Drake's translation, p. 102. On Galileo's Platonism, see A. Koyré, 'Galileo and the Scientific Revolution of the Seventeenth Century', *Philosophical Review*, 52, 1943, pp. 333–48; 'Galileo and Plato', *Journal of the History of Ideas*, 1943, pp. 460–78. Both these articles are reprinted in *Metaphysics and Measurement*.
3 John Ray, *The Wisdom of God* (1691), third edition, 1701, p. 52.
4 *The True Intellectuall System of the Universe*, 1678, pp. 674, 676.
  to Gassendi. See, for example, ibid., p. 675.
5 Cudworth saw the story of '*Atomick Atheism*' as stretching from Epicurus
6 ibid., p. 683.
7 *Principles* I 58, 59.
8 'Though there is no doubt that the world could contain shapes such as those considered by geometers, I would deny that there are in fact any in our environment, except perhaps ones which are so small that they make no impression on our senses'; *Replies* V, AT VII 381; HR II 227.
9 Cf. *The World*, AT XI 3–6; *Dioptrics*, AT VI 85.
10 Platonistic theories of knowledge also enshrined the view that knowledge of the sensible world is particular or specific rather than universal or general. Sensory knowledge was supposed to be confined to species, which is why the word 'specious' came to mean the delusive appearances which things present to the senses. Cf. Dijksterhuis, *The Mechanisation of the World Picture*, p. 148. The notion of 'species' was also applied, by medieval philosophers, to the intelligible world: 'intelligible species' were counterparts to 'concepts'.
11 *Principles* I 45, 46.
12 ibid., 45.
13 *Rules* XII, AT X 427; HR I 46.
14 The connection between distinctness and the simple natures has been noticed by Kemp Smith ('The distinct ... coincides with the "simple"', *New Studies*, p. 58), and Alan Gewirth, 'Clearness and Distinctness in Descartes' (*Philosophy*, vol. XVIII, no. 69, 1943, pp. 17–36, reprinted in Doney (ed.), *Descartes*). See pp. 268–9 in Doney. Self-consistency is obviously necessary for distinctness. For instance, a right-angle triangle 'cannot be distinctly understood if the relation of equality between the squares of its sides and of its base is denied' (*Replies* IV, AT VII 225; AT IX 175; HR II 101).
15 *Meditations*, Synopsis, AT VII 13; AT IX 10; HR I 140–41. Here Descartes also refers to the propositions which spell out the natures of simple things – propositions like the *cogito* – as clear and distinct.
16 *Meditations* III, AT VII 46; AT IX 36; HR I 166.

Mind and Body

17 ibid., AT VII 43; AT IX 34; HR I 164.
18 ibid., AT VII 44; AT IX 34; HR I 164.
19 Cf. the four 'Rules of Method' in *Discourse* II, AT VI 18–19; HR I 192.
20 *Discourse* IV, AT VI 33; HR I 102; cf. *Meditations* III, AT VII 35; AT IX 27; HR I 158.
21 *Human Knowledge, its Scope and Limits*, p. 172.
22 The one exception to this principle is the idea of God (see above, p. 135); cf. *Replies* I, AT VII, 116–17; AT IX 92; HR II 20: 'We must distinguish between possible and necessary existence, and note that in the concept or idea of everything that is clearly and distinctly conceived, possible existence is contained, but necessary existence never, except in the idea of God alone.' See also letter to Mersenne, iii 42; 'You attribute to me, as an axiom of mine, *that everything we conceive clearly is, or exists*. My view is not this at all; it is only that everything we perceive clearly is true, and so exists if we perceive that it is impossible for it not to exist; otherwise that it can exist if we perceive that its existence is possible.' See also *Discourse* IV, AT VI 36; HR I 103–4.
23 *Meditations* III, AT VII 43; AT IX 34; HR I 164.
24 ibid., AT VII 43–4; AT IX 34–5; HR I 164. The passage in brackets is in French only.
25 *Meditations* II, AT VII 31; AT IX 24–5; HR I 155.
26 *Replies* V, AT VII 371; HR II 220.
27 *Discourse* IV, AT VI 33; HR I 102.

9 MIND AND BODY

1 *Meditations* VI, AT VII 81; AT IX 64; HR I 192; *Principles* I 71.
2 Descartes's statements about the ordinary language of human action and perception were extremely confusing; and his suggestions as to how it might be improved unsystematic and inconsistent. For example he said that he made no distinction between seeing things and thinking one is seeing things (*Meditations* II, AT VII 33; AT IX 26; HR I 156). And sometimes he suggested that the word 'sensation' should be applied to purely physical states of the body, while at other times he suggested exactly the opposite, that it should only be applied to thoughts. For instance at one point in the Second Meditation he said that 'it is impossible to have sensations unless one has a body' while at another he said that 'what is strictly called "sensing"' is the judgements people make on the basis of sensory experience. Although such judgements were 'nothing other than thinking' they had to be called 'sensations' because 'people are accustomed to ascribing them to the senses' (*Meditations* II, AT VII 27; AT IX 21; HR I 151; ibid., AT VII 29; HR I 153; *Replies* VI, AT VII 438; AT IX 237; HR II 252).
3 Cf. Descartes's view that gravitation could not be explained by means

of the concept of attraction, because attraction was a concept which could only be applied in relation to beings which could think. *Replies* VI, AT VII 441; AT IX 240; HR II 255. See above pp. 53-54.

4 *Meditations* VI, AT VII 83; AT IX 66; HR I 194.

5 In this context, Descartes used the word 'intellect' in a narrower sense than when he used it as a synonym for 'mind'.

6 *Meditations* III, AT VII 37; AT IX 29; HR I 159.

7 *Meditations* IV, AT VII 56; AT IX 45; HR I 174. The passage in brackets is in French only; its message is reiterated in *Replies* V (letter to Clerselier), AT IX 206; HR II 127, and in a letter to Mersenne, 22 vii 41.

8 *Meditations* III, AT VII 43; AT IX 34; HR I 164.

9 *Meditations* II, AT VII 32; AT IX 25; HR I 155-6. See also *Principles* I 9.

10 Leibniz, however, wrote that 'Descartes' main merit was to revive the Platonistic tendency to lead the mind away from the senses'. See H. Gouhier, *La Pensée Métaphysique*, p. 52, n. 63.

11 Most modern accounts of Descartes's theory of sensation interpret it as a form of pluralism. They present it not as an attempt to advance an original theory about the role of thought in sensation but as an early example of the extended use of words like 'mind' and 'mental'. In the service of this interpretation, they have to say that Descartes also tried to extend the meaning of the word 'thought' (*cogitatio, pensée*) to make it cover things like physical sensations. As a result, some translators have used words like 'consciousness', 'awareness' or even 'experience' to translate Descartes's words for thought (Anscombe and Geach use all these translations: see p. xlvii of their translation; see also Keeling, *Descartes*, p. 168; Kenny, *Descartes*, p. 69). But as Kenny admits when he advances this pluralist interpretation, if he is right then 'French and Latin usage were never as wide as that to be found in Descartes' (Kenny, pp. 68-9; see also Russell, *My Philosophical Development*, Allen & Unwin, 1959, p. 25). Such accounts as these have the implausible implication that Descartes was not particularly keen on 'separating the mind from the senses'. Thus Bennett is led to claim that Descartes made the mistake of regarding 'concepts and sensory states as species of a single genus' (Jonathan Bennett, *Kant's Analytic*, Cambridge University Press, 1966, p. 55. Perhaps the source of this view is that Descartes is seen as resembling Locke; for Bennett also says, 'Descartes and Locke used the word "idea" to stand indifferently for sense data and for what one "has in mind" when one thinks or understands.'). Similarly Kenny remarks that Descartes made the mistake of 'identifying sensation with thought'. Kenny also suggests that Descartes would have regarded headaches and pangs of hunger as examples of thoughts (Kenny, pp. 71, 69. Kenny bases his case partly on a misleading translation: he puts 'has a sense or thought of itself seeing' for '*sentit sive cogitat se videre*', p. 72). In implying that Descartes was trying to blur the distinction between mental and

physical states, these claims go against one of the firmest points in the interpretation of Descartes. The only passages which might appear to justify the pluralistic interpretation of Descartes's account of the mind are those where Descartes expressed genuine hesitation about the possibility of completely disentangling mental and physical states. In the Sixth Meditation, for instance, he seems to have wanted to say that it was impossible to completely replace ordinary hybrid descriptions of human action and perception with descriptions of thinking on the one hand and of matter in motion on the other. He spoke in an uncharacteristically metaphorical way about how in human beings mind and matter were 'intermingled ... to form ... one whole' (*Meditations* VI, AT VII 81; AT IX 64; HR I 192). He continued this line of thought in the sixth *Replies*, where he suggested that there is a type or aspect of sensation which cannot be reduced either to a person's physical states or to his mental states (*Replies* VI, AT VII 436–9; AT IX 236–8; HR II 251–3). But even when he made remarks like these Descartes was not saying that things other than thoughts ought to be ascribed to the mind. For the fact that such states could not conceivably exist without the body meant that a person's knowledge of them was not completely certain, and so, by Descartes's definition of the mind (see above, p. 96), that they were not mental. As Descartes put it (presupposing the identity of himself and his mind) 'I can apprehend myself as complete without them' (*Meditations* VI, AT VII 78; AT IX 62; HR I 190). Thus there is no reason to suppose that Descartes ever wavered in his conviction that all mental operations can be reduced to thinking. (See above, p. 180, note 2, for an account of Descartes's inconsistent use of words like 'sensation'.) For further discussion, see Zeno Vendler, *Res Cogitans*, Ithaca, N.Y., Cornell University Press, 1972, ch. 7.

12 According to Wittgenstein, toothache is a 'mental state, meaning a state of consciousness' (*Blue Book*, p. 18).

13 *Meditations* II, AT VII 31; AT IX 25; HR I 155.

14 See for example Locke's *Essay*, Two XIX 1; XIX 4; VII 1. Cf. Aaron, *John Locke*, p. 131.

15 Their anti-psychologism can be traced back to Kant. See for example *Prolegomena to any Future Metaphysics*, para. 21a, p. 51.

16 *Grundgesetze der Arithmetic*, 1893, p. xiv. Husserl's anti-psychologism is explained in *Cartesian Meditations*, para. 17.

17 'On Sense and Reference', Geach and Black, p. 61. Frege added that whereas thought was objective, imagery was completely private and incommunicable: 'A man never has somebody else's mental image, but only his own; and nobody knows how far his image (say) of red agrees with someone else's.' Review quoted in Geach and Black, p. 70.

18 Cf. Wittgenstein's definition: 'Psychological verbs are characterised by

the fact that the third person of the present is to be verified by observation, the first person not.' *Zettel*, 472.

19 *Meditations*, Synopsis, AT VII 12; AT IX 9; HR I 140.

20 *Principles* I 9.

21 *Meditations* II, AT VII 27; AT IX 21; HR I 151. See also *Passions* 26.

22 'In them there can be no falsity'; *Replies* VI, AT VII 438; AT IX 237; HR II 252.

23 Letter to Plempius for Fromondus, 3 x 37.

24 '*Intellectu*', '*Entendement*'. *Replies* VI, AT VII 438; AT IX 237; HR II 252.

25 *Meditations* II, AT VII 29; AT IX 23; HR I 153.

26 *Meditations* VI, AT VII 77; AT IX 61; HR I 189.

27 *La Phénoménologie de la Perception*, p. 96.

28 It is interesting that one of Freud's attempts to differentiate the unconscious from the preconscious was based on this criterion. In *The Ego and the Id*, ch. 2 (*Collected Works*, vol. XIX, p. 20) he said that a thing entered the preconscious by 'becoming connected with the image of the word corresponding to it'.

29 'To be united to the body is not to the detriment of the soul but for its enrichment. There is the substantial benefit of completing human nature, and the accidental benefit of achieving knowledge that can only be acquired through the senses'; *Disputationes de Anima*, 1 ad 7, 2 ad 14; Gilby 543.

10 DUALISM AND MATERIALISM

1 Descartes himself wrote that although the mind is not part of the physical world it could still be called 'physical' since it interacted with physical things. Letter to Hyperaspistes, viii 41; cf. letter to Elisabeth, 28 vi 43; to Arnauld, 29 vii 48. See H. Gouhier, *La Pensée Métaphysique*, pp. 360–63.

2 Andrew Marvell (1621–78), 'A Dialogue Between the Soul and Body'.

3 Cf. G. E. M. Anscombe's lecture, *Causality and Determination*, Cambridge University Press, 1971, p. 26.

4 As far as I know, Leibniz's interpretation is a conjecture with no direct textual support. Leibniz's statement ran as follows: 'Descartes saw that souls cannot by any means import force to bodies, because there is always the same quantity of force in matter. Yet he thought that the soul could change the direction of bodies. This, however, was because at the time the law of nature which affirms also the conservation of the same total direction in the motion of matter was not known. If he had known that law, he would have fallen upon my system of pre-established harmony.' *Monadology*, 1714, 80; Gerhardt, vol. VI, pp. 620–621. See also *Nouveaux Essais*, 1704, book II, ch. 23, para. 28; Gerhardt, vol. V, pp. 208–9.

5 Marx and Engels, *The Holy Family*, p. 169.

6 *Le Philosophe Ignorant*, 1766, section 13.

7 Early examples of such conjectures can be found in Hobbes, *Objections III*, AT VII 172–3; AT IX 134; HR II 61; and in Locke, *Essay*, Four III. For later examples, see Cassirer, *The Philosophy of the Enlightenment*, pp. 66, 68.

8 Cf. Aram Vartanian, 'Trembly's Polyp, La Mettrié, and Eighteenth-Century French Materialism', in Wiener and Noland (eds.), *Roots of Scientific Thought*, New York: Basic Books, 1957, pp. 497–516. See also Aram Vartanian, *Diderot and Descartes*, ch. 4, especially p. 211.

9 In 1646, Le Roy (otherwise known as Regius) produced a short and popular textbook of Cartesian physics, the *Fundamenta Physicis*, which overshadowed Descartes's *Principles*, and excited considerable jealousy and hatred in Descartes. Cf. Mouy, *Le Développement de la Physique Cartésienne 1646–1712*, pp. 73, 90.

10 *Notae in Programma*, AT VIII 342; HR I 432.

11 ibid., AT VIII 350; HR I 437.

12 Cf. Wittgenstein, *Tractatus*, 4.011.

13 Obviously they would be adequate in conjunction with a rule for translating the reductive description into a structural specification.

14 *Essay*, Four III 6.

15 Cf. Donald Davidson, 'Mental Events' in Foster and Swanson (eds.), *Experience and Theory*, Amherst, Ma., University of Massachusetts Press, 1970, pp. 79–102.

16 Ryle, *The Concept of Mind*, pp. 11, 15–16.

17 A relation is external, as opposed to internal, if and only if each of the things it holds between can be identified without reference to the other.

18 *Meditations VI*, AT VII 86; AT IX 69; HR I 196.

19 ibid., AT VII 81; AT IX 64; HR I 192.

II THE IMMORTAL SOUL

1 Cf. Geach, *God and the Soul*, pp. 17–18.

2 *The Golden Bough*, p. 874.

3 Cf. Bruno Snell, *The Discovery of the Mind*, p. 9.

4 Cf. G. S. Brett, *A History of Psychology*, p. 44.

5 ibid., p. 219.

6 Quoted in E. R. Dodds, *The Greeks and the Irrational*, p. 135.

7 Cf. Brett, op. cit., p. 314.

8 *Meditations II*, AT VII 26; AT IX 20; HR I 152.

9 *Summa Contra Gentiles* II 81; cf. ibid., IV 79: 'This soul is commensurate with this body, not with that, that soul with that body, and so with all of them.'

10 The problem was particularly difficult given Aquinas's view that a disembodied soul could not even think of sensible particulars. See above p. 98.

11 It has been suggested by Chomsky (in *Cartesian Linguistics*, New York, Harper & Row, 1966, pp. 3–6) that Descartes's comparison of animals and automata with men in terms of their linguistic capacities represents a serious argument for his opinion. But this suggestion is unconvincing. In his letter to More of 5 ii 49, for example, Descartes says that 'it has never yet been observed, that any brute animal reached the stage of using real speech, that is to say, of indicating by word or sign something pertaining to pure thought and not to natural impulse', but admits that this is not a *proof* that animals do not think.

12 *Discourse* IV, AT VI 33; HR I 101.

13 Another attack on idealism could be launched on the basis of the view, put forward by writers like Wittgenstein, Geach, Prior and Strawson, that thoughts whose expression essentially involves singular terms can only be specified if their particular context is indicated demonstratively.

14 Gilson, *Études sur le Rôle de la Pensée Médiévale*, p. 215.

15 An example of this twilight sense is the sense of the conjunction of premisses of a *reductio ad absurdum* proof.

16 This view was based in turn on the theory that all spatio-temporal descriptions could be translated into non-spatio-temporal descriptions.

17 *Nouveaux Essais*, preface; Gerhardt, vol. V, p. 51.

18 Relying on an idiosyncratic theory of meaning, Spinoza was able to say that the identity of minds was rigidly co-ordinated with that of bodies: minds and bodies were complementary aspects of an underlying substance, identified with God or nature. However, Spinoza's Cartesian physics, with its denial of vacuum, caused him doubts about the possibility of individuating bodies.

19 Averroes was a medieval Arabic philosopher who was very influential in Padua and Paris. Averroism was pronounced a heresy by the Lateran Council in 1513.

20 'The savage, unshackled by dogma, is free to explain the facts of life by the assumption of as many souls as he thinks necessary'; Frazer, *The Golden Bough*, p. 903.

21 See AT III 513.

22 *Meditations*, Dedication, AT VII 3; AT IX 5–6; HR I 134–5; *Replies* VII, AT VII 549; HR II 335.

23 See above, 7 note 6, p. 177.

24 Letter to Villebressieu, summer 1631, AT I 216.

25 *Principles* I 63.

26 'Descartes' Philosophy of Nature is rigorously monistic; his Philosophy of Mind alone is pluralistic'; Keeling, *Descartes*, p. 145, n. 1; cf. p. 130, n. 1.

27 *Entretien avec Burman*, AT V 156.

28 This is probably the source of Descartes's attempt to distinguish between ideas and thoughts, by describing ideas as the 'forms' of thoughts (*Replies* II, AT VII 160; AT IX 124; HR II 52).

29 *Meditations*, Synopsis, AT VII 14; AT IX 10; HR I 141.

30 Descartes adds that strictly speaking God is the only substance; *Principles* I 51.

31 Cf. letters to Mersenne, 24 xii 40, 31 xii 40.

32 *Meditations*, Synopsis, AT VII 14 (without the phrase in brackets); AT IX 10; HR I 141.

12 FREEDOM AND ACTION

1 *Principles*, Letter to the Translator, AT IX (ii) 4; HR I 205.

2 It is hard, however, to give a precise and detailed account of the concepts of action and passion. (a) A can be active in relation to B but passive in relation to C. For example, if rain acts on limestone to produce curiously shaped outcrops, the rain is active and the limestone is passive; but if wind makes the rain fall at a slant, the wind is active and the rain is passive. (b) In relation to what can loosely be called one and the same process, it may be possible to say both that A is active in relation to B and that B is active in relation to A. For example, if a thunderbolt falls out of the sky, and has its fall broken by trees, then the thunderbolt acted on the trees, bending its branches, and the trees acted on the falling thunderbolt, slowing down its descent.

As the last example shows, which element one regards as active and which as passive depends on how one describes the process. Normally processes are described in terms of their results, but often one can describe the results in various ways. (Strictly, however, it is perhaps misleading to speak of the same process under different descriptions.) In general, the object from whose point of view the results are described is regarded as passive. If one describes it from the point of view of the tree (having its branches bent) then the tree is passive; if one describes it from the point of view of the thunderbolt (having its fall broken) then the thunderbolt is passive.

Choices between different ways of describing processes are not a matter of indifference. Their guiding principle depends on which item associated with the process is regarded as the cause of the process. The process is then described from the point of view of the effects which this cause has, and so the cause appears as active. But what does it mean to call something the *cause* of a process, and hence to think of it as active? The following suggestions might be made, but they are all inadequate. (a) That the presence of the active element is necessary for the process to occur, whereas the presence of the passive one is not. This suggestion must be wrong because both agent and patient are essential: for example the rain could not produce outcrops if the limestone was not there to be acted on. (b) That the character of the results of the process depends on the agent more than on the patient. But in the case of the limestone the opposite is true: the character of the limestone formation depends more on the original shape and composition of the limestone than on anything about the rain. (c) That the agent exists before the patient, or that its action occurs before the patient's passion. This suggestion must be wrong because in producing the outcrops the limestone and the rain are involved simultaneously. The justification for calling one element in a process the cause depends on much less easily statable principles; and very often, it depends on a highly abstract theory, such as the principle of inertia (see above, pp 118-119).

3 Cf. Leibniz, *Discourse on Metaphysics* XV.

4 (My emphasis) *The World* VII, AT XI 43-4; cf. *Principles* II 34.

5 Cf. *Passions* 28.

6 Letter to Regius, v 41.

7 *Meditations* IV, AT VII 58; AT IX 46; HR I 175.

8 *Pensées*, 346, 348.

9 This view is to be distinguished from the Humean view that 'moral good and evil belong only to the actions of the mind' (*Treatise*, III i 1); for Descartes could consistently have claimed that ethical inquiry was concerned with other things besides the moral character of thinking beings.

10 In *The Concept of Mind*, for instance, Ryle assumes that the mental is a special concern of the moralist (p. 204).

11 'The State of Funk', *Selected Essays*, Penguin Books, 1950, p. 100.

12 Lawrence goes on to say, 'You have to accept sex fully in the consciousness. Accept sex fully in the consciousness, and let the normal physical awareness come back'; ibid., pp. 101–2.

13 *Life Against Death*, 1959, Sphere Books, 1968, p. 19.

14 Cf. *Meditations* III, AT VII 36; AT IX 39; HR I 159. See above pp. 92–94.

15 *Passions* 16; cf. 13 and 33. Cf. *Replies* IV, AT VII 229; AT IX 178; HR II 103.

16 Passages like this have led Descartes to be widely credited with inventing the concept of a reflex action. But this is an exaggeration, since Descartes thought of reflex actions as depending on the brain. Cf. G. Canguilhem, *La Formation du Concept de Réflexe*, esp. pp. 37ff.

17 Cf. *Passions* 36.

18 *Passions* 50.

19 *Passions* 46.

20 *Passions* 25. In the *Passions*, Descartes confined his attention to passions which were 'related to the soul itself'; the six 'primary' ones being wonder, love, hatred, desire, joy and sadness. *Passions* 69.

21 One result of the ambiguity of Descartes's theory was that it made him use the word 'will' in two different ways. Sometimes he applied it to an element present in all thoughts (to actions in the homunculus sense) and sometimes to an element present only in some thoughts (to actions in the dualist sense). Thus in the Third Meditation, Descartes spoke of the will as involved in all thoughts (*Meditations* III, AT VII 37; AT IX 29; HR I 159; see above pp. 92–93). He was particularly anxious to say that the will is involved in the perception of external objects and bodily states, because he thought that these were often erroneous and that error always depended on the will. Hence it was involved in both the actions and passions of the soul, as these were conceived on the dualist theory. But Descartes also thought of the will as being involved only in actions and not in passions, so that in *Passions* 18 he said that perceptions did not involve the will at all.

13 THE INNER SELF

1 Karl Marx, *Capital*, vol. I, part I, ch. 2, p. 84.

2 *Second Treatise of Government*, section 27.

3 *Leviathan*, ch. 24.

4 'On Christian Liberty', quoted in Hegel's *Philosophy of Right*, section 48.

5 'The division between the personal and the class individual, the accidental nature of the conditions of life for the individual, appears only with the emergence of the class, which is itself a product of the bourgeoisie', Marx and Engels, *The German Ideology*, edited by C. J. Arthur, Lawrence & Wishart, 1970, p. 84.

6 Many of the ideas of this paragraph come from C. B. MacPherson's *The Political Theory of Possessive Individualism*, especially pp. 48–9, 142.

7 'A Contribution to the Critique ... Introduction', McLellan, ed., *Early Works*, p. 123.

8 'Take any action allow'd to be Vicious ... The vice entirely escapes you, as long as you consider the object. You never can find it, till you turn your reflection into your own breast ...' Hume, *Treatise*, III i 1.

9 'I coddle my heart like a sick child and give in to its every whim ...' Goethe, *Sorrows of Young Werther*, Book I.

10 'Nature has placed mankind under the governance of two sovereign masters, *pain* and *pleasure*. It is for them alone to point out what we ought to do ...' Bentham, *Fragment on Government*, ch. 1, section 1.

11 These themes are well discussed in Lionel Trilling's *Sincerity and Authenticity*, Oxford University Press, 1972, especially ch. 1. See also Ian Watt, *The Rise of the Novel* (1957), Penguin Books, 1963, ch. 6, especially pp. 180–83.

12 I am using the word 'self' as a name for the subject of such actions. The self might be called the 'tautological subject' of such acting, just as the

actions are its tautological object. Similarly, a winner is the tautological subject of winning, and a win or victory is its tautological object.

13 'Below the Surface Stream' (1869).

14 Shakespeare had used the phrase in *Hamlet* (I, ii, 185, also I, i, 112), though he was not quite the first to use it. But in these earlier uses, the only objects which the mind's eye could be said to see were objects of the type one sees with physical eyes. Descartes, in contrast, used the phrase in such a way that the mind's eye could be said to see abstract truths (*Meditations* III, AT VII 36; not in French or in HR).

15 *Essay*, Two XIX 3, 4.

16 *Essay*, Two VI.

17 *Le Rêve de d'Alembert* (1769), *Œuvres Philosophiques*, p. 339.

18 ibid., p. 346.

19 ibid., p. 347.

20 ibid., p. 348. This resembles Descartes's account of the 'power of the soul over the passions' in *Passions*, 45–6; see above, pp. 121-122.

21 Cf. Foucault, *Madness and Civilisation*, pp. 87–8.

22 Diderot, op. cit., p. 357.

23 Foucault, op. cit., p. 158.

24 '*Un fou est un malade dont le cerveau pâtit, comme le gouteux est un malade qui souffre aux pieds et aux mains . . . On a la goutte au cerveau comme aux pieds.*' Voltaire, *Dictionnaire Philosophique*, Article 'Folie'.

25 *Meditations* II (Title), AT VII 23; AT IX 18; HR I 149.

26 *Meditations*, Dedication, AT VII 5; AT IX 5; HR I 134.

27 *Meditations*, Synopsis, AT VII 16; AT IX 12; HR I 143.

28 *Replies* V, AT VII 360; HR II 215.

29 *Principles* I 11; cf. letter to Mersenne, July 1641: 'Since it is through it that we conceive all sorts of things, it is also more conceivable on its own than all other things together.'

30 *Meditations* III, AT VII 37; AT IX 29; HR I 159. My interpretation of this passage shows that it does not support the common allegation that Descartes held a 'resemblance theory of meaning', i.e. that he thought one could explain an idea's standing for an object or property in terms of its resembling it. The allegation is sometimes also based on some remarks in Descartes's early works, especially the *Dioptrics*. But what Descartes actually says in these works is that some (physical) ideas resemble what they stand for, and others – such as ideas of bodily pain – do not. He emphasized, however, that it was an error to suppose that we had little eyes inside our brains to look at these image-like ideas (*Dioptrics* VI, AT VI 130). 'The soul has no need to contemplate images which resemble the things it perceives . . .; nevertheless the objects we look at do in fact impress quite good likenesses of themselves on the backs of our eyes' (*Dioptrics* V, AT VI 114). According to Descartes's neurophysiological theories this likeness was then transmitted at least

in part to the animal spirits in the imagination. (To be specific, his neuro-physiology allowed for the transmission of shape, motion and relative size from the object to the imagination; and Descartes may well have thought that this supported his view that these are the physical pro-perties which are best known to human beings.) Descartes certainly does not say that it is neccesary for an idea to resemble what it stands for.

31 *Principles* I 19.

32 Letter to Mersenne, 28 i 41.

33 Cf. Richard Wollheim, 'The Mind and the Mind's Image of Itself', *International Journal of Psychoanalysis*, 1969.

34 'Notes for Lectures', p. 238.

35 Cf. Wittgenstein's comment on the senselessness of trying to give private names to one's sensations: 'I have no criterion of correctness. One would like to say: whatever is going to seem right to me is right. And this only means that here we can't talk about "right".' (*Philosophical Investigations* 258.)

36 'The Unconscious', *Complete Works*, vol. XIV, p. 171.

14 THE IDEA OF GOD

1 Cf. Gilson, *Comm.*, pp. 320–21.

2 *Meditations* III, AT VII 40; AT IX 31; HR I 162. The French translation contains the additional phrase, '*les considérant comme des images*', which suggests that the notion applies only to ideas in the intellect. See above, p. 132.

3 *Meditations* III, AT VII 40; AT IX 32; HR I 162.

4 For the sake of brevity, I have left out of account the distinction be-tween having reality 'eminently' and having it 'formally'; *Meditations* III, AT VII 41; AT IX 32; HR I 162.

5 ibid., AT VII 43; AT IX 34; HR I 164.

6 ibid., AT VII 42; AT IX 33; HR I 163.

7 One of Descartes's reasons for saying this is the claim that if a person could construct the idea, he would be identical with God; *Meditations* III, AT VII 46–7; HR I 167.

8 ibid., AT VII 51; AT IX 40; HR I 170.

9 ibid., AT VII 40; AT IX 32; HR I 162.

10 In his letter to Mesland, 2 v 44, Descartes said the second could be re-garded as an explanation of the first. See also *Replies* IV, AT VII 238; AT IX 184; HR II 109.

11 This interpretation is supported by Gouhier (*La Pensée Métaphysique*, ch. 6, esp. pp. 176–7), Hamelin (*Le Système de Descartes*, pp. 200, 214–16) and Gilson (*Comm.*, p. 351). Gilson says of the ontological argument: '*C'est une preuve où l'efficace du principe de causalité se trouve en quelque sorte ramassée à l'intérieur de l'essence divine.*'

12 '*Ad cujus solius essentiam existentia pertinet*'; '*en l'idée duquel seul l'existence nécessaire ou éternelle est comprise*'; AT VII 69; AT IX 55; HR I 183.

13 'Valley', i.e. downward slope. *Meditations* V, AT VII 66; AT IX 52; HR I 181.

14 *Critique of Pure Reason*, p. 507.

15 See above, Appendix 2, p. 162.

16 Cf. Marx's remark, 'The ontological proof amounts merely to this: What I really imagine is for me a real imagination.' *Early Texts*, p. 18.

17 '*In quo omnis realitas formaliter contineatur quae est in idea tantum objective*'; '*. . . dans ces idées*'; *Meditations* III, AT VII 42; AT IX 33; HR I 163.

18 'Notes for Lectures', p. 254; *Notebooks*, p. 85.

19 *Meditations* III, AT VII 45; AT IX 35–6; HR I 165. The words in brackets were absent from the Latin, but were intended by Descartes. Cf. Gilson, *Comm.*, pp. 333–4.

20 Cf. *Principles* I 28, Latin only; letter to Reneri for Pollot, April/May 1638.

21 *Pensées*, 77.

15 KNOWLEDGE AND HUMANISM

1 *Rules* XII, AT X 418; HR I 40–41.

2 Several passages in the later works can be interpreted as survivals of Descartes's earlier scepticism, such as *Replies* II, AT VII 145; AT IX 113–114; HR II 41.

3 The criticism is so well known that Descartes's argument is normally referred to as 'the Cartesian circle'. The first to make it was Arnauld, in *Objections* IV, AT VII 214; AT IX 166; HR II 92.

4 Descartes himself makes this point, but in a different context and apparently without realizing how much it damaged his argument: 'I cannot deny that, in a way, it is a greater perfection in the universe as a whole that some of its parts should not be free from error while others are true, than that they should all be exactly alike.' *Meditations* IV, AT VII 61; AT IX 49; HR I 178.

5 'There are in us seeds of knowledge (*semina scientiae*), just as there are seeds of fire in a flint: philosophers extract them by reasoning, while poets take possession of them by the imagination' (*Olympica*, AT X 217). 'Certain seeds of truth, laid down by nature in the human mind' (*Rules* IV, AT X 376; HR I 12; cf. AT X 373; HR I 10). See also *Discourse* VI, AT VI 64; HR I 121.

6 *Meditations* III, AT VII 51; AT IX 41; HR I 170.

7 *Meditations* V, AT VII 63; AT IX 50; HR I 179.

8 The examples are mind, matter, God, movement, duration, size and number. See above p. 88.

9 *Meditations* III, AT VII 40; AT IX 31; HR I 162.

10 This is partly due to the fact that he thought his theory of innate ideas followed from the rejection of the view that perception involves reception by the perceiver of something transmitted from the object perceived. Descartes rejected this view because it ignored 'the limitation of the senses and of what can penetrate through this medium to the mind'. All the sense-organs could do, he said, was 'transmit something which gives the mind occasion to form those ideas, by means of an innate faculty'. It followed that these ideas, even though they might be obscure and confused, were innate rather than received from objects. *Notes Against a Programme*, AT VIII 358; HR I 442–3; cf. *Replies* VI, AT VII 437; AT IX 236–7; HR II 251–2; letter to Mersenne, 22 vii 41.

11 *Notes Against a Programme*, AT VIII 357; HR I 442.

12 Clearly this theory of innate ideas has nothing to do with modern 'theories of innate ideas' which postulate innate capacities for language-learning.

13 (My emphasis) *Discourse* V, AT VI 40; HR I 106; cf. Gilson, *Comm.*, p. 372; cf. *The World: Treatise on Light*, AT XI 147. The same link is made in the letter to Mersenne of 15 iv 30.

14 Letter to Mersenne, 15 iv 30.

15 God is 'the author of the essence of created things as well as of their existence and the essence is nothing other than these eternal truths'; letter to Mersenne, 27 v 30.

16 *Discourse* V, AT VI 40; HR I 106.

17 Aquinas located eternal ideas or archetypes in the mind of God; while they depended on his nature, they did not depend on his will.

18 One way in which Aquinas expressed this view was in his remark that 'The question "What kind of thing is it?" comes after the question "Does it exist?"' (*Summa Theologiae*, 1a ii 2 ad 2). (Aquinas however had a distinction between real and nominal essence, and was here speaking only of the former, whereas the question of God's existence had to do with the latter. Descartes did not make any such distinction.) Descartes tried to abolish this dichotomy between essence and existence, pointing out that it is impossible to inquire into what exists without having some conception of what you are looking for – and this, according to Descartes, is a conception of its essence. 'According to true logic, one should never ask of a thing *whether it exists* without first knowing *what it is.*' *Replies* I, AT VII 167–8; AT IX 86; HR II 13. Cf. Hamelin's remark that the 'Cartesian revolution in logic' consisted in the replacement of a 'logic of extension' by a logic based on 'comprehension or connotation' (*Le Système de Descartes*, p. 89). See also Gilson, *Comm.*, pp. 184–5.

19 Spinoza, *Ethics*, Book I, appendix.

20 'Descartes' treatment of essences is exactly analogous in import to the treatment of Christ by the Socinians of his epoch. He humanises

essences, as they humanised Christ; and he thereby makes it possible for there to be human knowledge perfect of its kind, as they make possible Christian perfection and the imitation of Christ' (Émile Bréhier, 'La Création des vérités éternelles dans le système de Descartes', *Revue Philosophique de la France et de l'Étranger*, CXIII, 1937, pp. 15–29; reprinted in Bréhier, *La Philosophie et son passé*, pp. 103–24; and translated by Doney in Doney (ed.), *Descartes*, pp. 192–208). My quotation is from p. 202 of Doney's translation.

21 'All impossibility . . . exists only in our concept or thought, which is unable to conjoin ideas which contradict each other'; *Replies II*, AT VII 159; AT IX 119; HR II 46. See also *Meditations VI*, AT VII 78; AT IX 62; HR I 190. See also *Replies I*, AT VII 116; AT IX 91–2; HR II 19–20; *Replies II*, AT VII 132; AT IX 104; HR II 32; letter to Gibieuf, 19 i 42.

22 *Replies VII*, AT VII 520; HR II 313.

23 *Replies IV*, AT VII 226; AT IX 176; HR II 101–2.

24 Article on Edward Davenant, *Brief Lives*.

25 *Meditations*, Preface, AT VII 7; HR I 137.

26 When this was proved, he could assert that 'from the fact that I know of no other things that belong to my essence, it follows that there really is no other thing which does belong to it'; AT VII 7; HR I 137.

27 *Meditations V*, AT VII 66; AT IX 53; HR I 181. (I have added the word 'necessarily' because the context evidently requires it.)

28 *Meditations V*, AT VII 67; AT IX 53; HR I 182.

29 *The World* III, AT XI 11; see above p. 60.

30 Letter to Mersenne, 18 ii 41.

31 This interpretation has been worked out in detail by H. G. Frankfurt in his article 'Descartes' Validation of Reason', *American Philosophical Quarterly*, vol. II, no. 2, April 1965; reprinted in Doney (ed.), *Descartes*. Frankfurt has elaborated his interpretation in his book *Demons, Dreamers and Madmen*, New York, Bobbs-Merrill, 1970.

32 Apart from the passing reference in the *Discourse*, Descartes mentioned the theory in the *Replies*, but only either inadvertently or reluctantly; *Replies V*, AT VII 380; HR II 226; *Replies VI*, AT VII 431–6; AT IX 232–6; HR II 248–51.

33 The subtitle of one of Descartes's minor works, *The Search After Truth*, proclaimed that 'pure natural light, without the assistance of either Religion or Philosophy, can settle which opinions an honest man ought to hold'; AT X 495; HR I 305.

34 Letter to Mersenne, 15 iv 30.

35 Cf. Leibniz, *Discourse on Metaphysics* II.

36 Cf. letters to Mersenne, 21 iv 41; 2 v 44.

37 *Replies VI*, AT VII 432; AT IX 233; HR II 248.

38 *Theories of Surplus Value*, vol. I, p. 52.

39 Letter to Mersenne, 6 v 30.

16 DESCARTES AND HISTORY

1 'Le Cartésianisme était devenu la science même'; Paul Mouy, Le Développement de la Physique Cartésienne, p. 216.

2 ibid., p. 145.

3 *Pensées*, 76.

4 *Enchyridion Metaphysicum*, London, 1671, preface. This passage is quoted and translated by Vartanian in *Diderot and Descartes*, p. 51. Earlier in his life, More (1614–87) had been a correspondent of Descartes's. Similar English reactions to Descartes by Cudworth and Ray have been quoted above, pp. 85–86.

5 *Principia*, book III, General Scholium, p. 546. Newton does not mention Descartes in this passage, but it is fairly certain that he had him in mind. Cf. Vartanian, *Diderot and Descartes*, p. 82.

6 For an account of the persecution of Cartesianism in France, see P. Bouillier, *Histoire de la Philosophie Cartésienne*, vol. I, pp. 452–72. Bouillier's work is unusual in that it presents Descartes as a great apologist for Christianity.

7 Gabriel Daniel, *Voyage du Monde de M. Descartes*, Paris 1691. This passage is quoted in Mouy, op. cit., p. 168.

8 Preface to Dudley North, *Discourses upon Trade*, London, 1691. This work is mentioned in K. Marx, *Capital*, vol. I, p. 390, n. 1.

9 M. Thomas, *Éloge Académique de Descartes*, Paris, 1765, pp. 7, 8.

10 *Discourse* VI, AT VI 70; HR I 124–5.

11 *Encyclopédie*, Discours Préliminaire, p. xxvi.

12 Cf. J. Laird, 'Descartes et la philosophie anglaise', *Revue Philosophique*, 1937, pp. 226–56. But it is interesting that Sprat, the author of the *History of the Royal Society* (1667), though not a scientist himself, could see nothing important in Descartes's method, saying that it was 'more allowable in matters of contemplation, and in a Gentleman, whose chief aim is his own delight . . . It can by no means stand with a practical and universal Inquiry.'

13 Cajori, Appendix to Newton's *Principia*, p. 629.

14 ibid., pp. 629–32.

15 *Essay* Four III 25; Four III 6.

16 'Éloge de Newton', quoted by Vartanian, op. cit., p. 141.

17 *Éléments de Philosophie* VI. Quoted by Cassirer, *The Philosophy of the Enlightenment*, p. 56.

18 Quoted by Cassirer, op. cit., p. 64.

19 *Pensées*, 52.

20 *Élémens de la Philosophie de Newton*, p. 16; cf. *Lettres Philosophiques* (1734), XIV, XV, XVI.

21 Colin MacLaurin, *An Account of Sir Isaac Newton's Philosophical Discoveries*, pp. 70–71. Quoted by E. W. Strong in 'Newtonian Explications

Appendix 1

of Natural Philosophy', *Journal for the History of Ideas*, 1957, pp. 49–83.
22 *Traité des Systèmes* (1749), quoted in Peter Gay, *The Enlightenment*, Vol 1, p. 139.
23 'Dissertation and Preliminary Notes' (1839). *Early Texts*, pp. 21–2.
24 Milhaud, *Descartes Savant*, p. 212. Ironically, Descartes used almost the same words to criticize other scientists. *Regulae* IV, AT X 380; HR I 15.
25 L. Roth, *Descartes' Discourse on Method*, pp. 96–7, 87. Other examples of this attitude have been quoted in earlier chapters, and many other examples could be given. A rare antidote to it is to be found in the essays by E. Denissoff collected in his *Descartes: Premier théoricien de la physique mathématique*.

APPENDIX I

1 *Rules* VI, AT X 381–2; HR I 15–16.
2 *Rules* VI, AT X 382; HR I 16. Descartes gives an example: 'Though the universal is more absolute than the particular in that it has a more simple nature, it could be said to be more relative in that it depends on individuals.'
3 L. J. Beck, *The Method of Descartes*, p. 71. Beck's entire interpretation of the method is based on this identification of criteria of absolutes with examples of simples. It leads to his eccentric denial that Descartes's *mathesis universalis* is a form of mathematics, and his suggestion that instead it is an account of what he mystifyingly calls 'the deductive process in which the simple natures enter as links in implicatory sequences'; op. cit., pp. 195–6.
4 The same double mistake is made in, e.g. Hartland-Swann's 'Descartes' "Simple Natures"', *Philosophy*, XXII, July 1947, p. 139, n. 1: 'There is little coherence,' he says, 'between the simple natures of *Rules* VI, and *Rules* XII.' See also S. V. Keeling, 'Le Réalisme de Descartes', *Revue de Métaphysique et de Morale*, 1937, pp. 75–6; *Descartes*, pp. 69–70.
5 *Meditations* I, AT VII 20; AT IX 15; HR I 146.
6 *Rules* XIV, AT X 438; HR 54–5.

APPENDIX 2

1 *Critique of Pure Reason*, pp. 500–507.
2 Cf. *Objections* V (Gassendi), AT VII 323; HR II 186; and Hume, *Dialogues concerning Natural Religion*, IX; Gilbert Ryle, 'Mr. Collingwood and the Ontological Argument', *Mind*, XLIV, no. 174, April 1935, pp. 137–51; P. F. Strawson, *The Bounds of Sense*, Methuen, 1966, p. 225.
An Introduction of Wittgenstein's Tractatus, third edition, Hutchinson, 1967, p. 15.
4 *Descartes*, ch. 7, esp. pp. 155–6, 168–9, 'Descartes' Ontological

Argument' in *Fact and Existence*, edited by J. Margolis, Oxford, Blackwell, 1969, pp. 18–36.

5 In fact, Meinongism would never try to justify inferences from 'secondary' to 'primary' existence.

6 There is an excellent discussion of these issues in J. M. Hinton's article, 'Quantification, Meinongism, and the Ontological Argument', *Philosophical Quarterly*, vol. xxii, no. 87, April 1972, pp. 97–109.

Select Bibliography

A. WORKS BY DESCARTES

Œuvres de Descartes (twelve volumes and supplement), edited by Charles Adam and Paul Tannery, Paris, Léopold Cerf, 1897–1913 ('AT').

The Philosophical Works of Descartes (two volumes), edited and translated by Elisabeth S. Haldane and G. R. T. Ross, Cambridge University Press, 1911–12 ('HR').

Descartes' Philosophical Writings, edited and translated by Norman Kemp Smith, Macmillan, 1952.

Descartes: Philosophical Writings, edited and translated by Elizabeth Anscombe and Peter Thomas Geach, Edinburgh, Nelson, 1954.

Descartes' Philosophical Letters, edited and translated by Anthony Kenny, Oxford University Press, 1970. (This contains most of the letters referred to.)

Sebba, G., *Bibliographia Cartesiana: A Critical Guide to the Descartes Literature, 1800–1960*, The Hague, Martinus Nijhoff, 1964, is an indispensable source of bibliographical information.

B. BOOKS

Aaron, R. I., *John Locke* (1937), Oxford University Press, 1955.

Aquinas, Thomas, *Philosophical Texts*, edited and translated by Thomas Gilby, Oxford University Press, 1951 ('Gilby').

Baillet, Adrien, *Vie de M. Descartes* (1691), Paris, La Table Ronde, 1946.

Beck, L. J., *The Method of Descartes*, Oxford University Press, 1952.

Bouillier, F., *Histoire de la Philosophie Cartésienne* (two volumes), Paris, 1854.

Brett, C. S., *A History of Psychology*, George Allen, 1912.

Buchdahl, G., *Metaphysics and the Philosophy of Science*, Oxford, Blackwell, 1969.

Burtt, E. A., *Metaphysical Foundations of Modern Physical Science* (1924), Routledge, 1932.

Canguilhem, G., *La Formation du concept de réflexe aux XVIIe et XVIIIe siècles*, Paris, Presses Universitaires de France, 1955.

Cassirer, Ernst, *The Philosophy of the Enlightenment* (1932), translated by C. A. Koelln and J. P. Pettegrove, Boston, Mass., Beacon Press, 1955.

Denissoff, E., *Descartes: Premier théoricien de la physique mathématique*, Louvain, Université de Louvain, 1970.

Dodds, E. R., *The Greeks and the Irrational*, Berkeley, Cal., University of California Press, 1951.

Select Bibliography

Diderot, Denis, Œuvres Philosophiques, edited by P. Vernière, Paris, Garnier, 1971.

Dijksterhuis, E. J., The Mechanisation of the World Picture (1950), translated by C. Dikshoorn, Oxford University Press, 1961.

Doney, W. (ed.), Descartes, Macmillan, 1968.

Foucault, Michel, Madness and Civilisation (1961), Tavistock, 1967.

Frazer, J. G., The Golden Bough (abridged edition), Macmillan, 1957.

Frege, G., Translations from the Philosophical Writings of Gottlob Frege, edited and translated by P. Geach and M. Black, Oxford, Blackwell, 1966.

Galileo, Dialogue concerning the Two Chief World Systems (1632), translated by Stillman Drake, Berkeley, Cal., University of California Press, 1953.

Dialogues concerning Two New Sciences (1638), translated by H. Crew and A. de Salvio (1914), New York, Dover, 1954.

Gay, Peter, The Enlightenment: an Interpretation (two volumes), Weidenfeld & Nicolson, 1967, 1970.

Geach, P. T., God and the Soul, Routledge & Kegan Paul, 1969.

Gilson, E., La Philosophie au Moyen Âge, Payot, Paris, 1925.

Études sur le rôle de la pensée médiévale dans la formation du système Cartésien, Paris, Vrin, 1930.

Discours de la méthode: Texte et commentaire (Comm.), fourth edition, Paris, Vrin, 1967.

Gouhier, H., Les Premières Pensées de Descartes, Paris, Vrin, 1958.

La Pensée Métaphysique de Descartes, Paris, Vrin, 1962.

Hamelin, O., Le Système de Descartes, second edition, Paris, Alcan, 1921.

Herivel, J., The Background to Newton's Principia, Oxford University Press, 1965.

Husserl, E., Cartesian Meditations, translated by Dorion Cairns, The Hague, Martinus Nijhoff, 1970.

Kant, I., Prolegomena to any Future Metaphysics (1783), translated by L. W. Beck, Manchester, Manchester University Press, 1953.

Critique of Pure Reason, translated by Norman Kemp Smith, Macmillan, 1929.

Keeling, S. V., Descartes (1934), Oxford University Press, 1968.

Kenny, A. J. P., Descartes: A Study of His Philosophy, New York, Random House, 1968.

Koyré, A., Études Galiléennes (1935-7), Paris, Hermann, 1966.

Études Newtoniennes, Paris, Gallimard, 1968.

Metaphysics and Measurement, Chapman & Hall, 1968.

Leibniz, G. W. von, Die philosophischen Schriften (seven volumes), edited by C. J. Gerhardt, Berlin, 1875-90.

MacPherson, C. B., The Political Theory of Possessive Individualism, Oxford University Press, 1962.

Select Bibliography

Marx, K., *Capital* (three volumes), translated by S. Moore and M. Aveling, Moscow, 1965, 1967, 1971.

Early Texts, edited and translated by D. McLellan, Oxford, Blackwell, 1971.

Marx, K., and Engels, F., *The Holy Family* (1845), translated by R. Dixon, Moscow, 1956.

Merleau-Ponty, M., *La Phénoménologie de la Perception*, Paris, Gallimard, 1945.

Milhaud, Gaston, *Descartes Savant*, Paris, Alcan, 1921.

Mouy, P., *Le Développement de la Physique Cartésienne 1646-1712*, Paris, Vrin, 1934.

Newton, I., *Principia Mathematica*, translated by A. Motte, revised by F. Cajori, Berkeley, Cal., University of California Press, 1934.

Opticks (1704), New York, Dover, 1952.

Roth, L., *Descartes' Discourse on Method*, Oxford University Press, 1937.

Russell, B., *Human Knowledge: Its Scope and Limits*, Unwin, 1948.

Ryle, G., *The Concept of Mind*, Hutchinson, 1949.

Sabra, A. I., *Theories of Light from Descartes to Newton*, Oldbourne, 1967.

Scott, J. F., *The Scientific Work of René Descartes*, Taylor & Francis, 1952.

Smith, Norman Kemp, *Studies in the Cartesian Philosophy*, Macmillan, 1902.

New Studies in the Philosophy of Descartes, Macmillan, 1953.

Snell, B., *The Discovery of the Mind: Greek Origins of European Thought*, translated by T. C. Rosenmayer (1953), New York, Harper & Row, 1960.

Spinoza, B., *Opera* (four volumes), edited by J. Van Vloten and J. P. N. Land, The Hague, 1914.

Vartanian, A., *Diderot and Descartes: A Study of Scientific Naturalism in the Enlightenment*, Princeton, N.J., Princeton University Press, 1953.

La Mettrie's 'L'Homme Machine', Princeton, N.J., Princeton University Press, 1960.

Voltaire, F. M. A. de, *Élémens de la Philosophie de Newton*, Amsterdam, 1738.

Vuiljemin, J., *Mathématiques et Métaphysique chez Descartes*, Paris, Presses Universitaires de France, 1960.

Weisheipl, J. A., *The Development of Physical Theory in the Middle Ages*, Sheed & Ward, 1959.

Wittgenstein, L., *Philosophical Investigations*, translated by G. E. M. Anscombe, second edition, Oxford, Blackwell, 1958.

The Blue and Brown Books, Oxford, Blackwell, 1958.

Zettel, edited and translated by G. E. M. Anscombe and G. H. von Wright, Oxford, Blackwell, 1967.

Notebooks 1914-1916, Oxford, Blackwell, 1969.

'Notes for Lectures on "Private Experiences" and "Sense Data"', edited by Rush Rhees (first published in *Philosophical Review*, LXXVII,

1968), reprinted in *The Private Language Argument,* edited by O. R. Jones, Macmillan, 1971, pp. 229-75.

C. ARTICLES

Blackwell, R. J., 'Descartes' Laws of Motion', *Isis,* 1960, pp. 220-34.
Dubarle, D., 'Sur la notion de quantité de mouvement', in *Mélanges Alexandre Koyré,* vol. II, edited by I. B. Cohen, Paris, Hermann, 1964.
Gabbey, A., 'Force and Inertia in Seventeenth-Century Dynamics', *Studies in History and Philosophy of Science,* May 1971.
Gouhier, H., 'Pour une histoire des méditations métaphysiques', *Revue des Sciences Humaines,* 1951.

Index